D1571981

Reshaping the Self

Reshaping the Self

Reflections on Renewal through Therapy

Michael Eigen, Ph.D.

PSYCHOSOCIAL PRESS
Madison   Connecticut

Library of Congress Cataloging-in-Publication Data

Eigen, Michael.
    Reshaping the self : reflections on renewal through therapy / Michael Eigen.
        p.   cm.
    Includes bibliographical references.
    ISBN 1-887841-00-8
    1. Psychotherapy—Case studies. 2. Self-actualization (Psychology)—Case studies. I. Title.
RC465.E343   1995
616.89'14—dc20   95-40586
                                            CIP

Manufactured in the United States of America

*To all engaged
by mysteries of renewal*

Like St. Augustine, my heart exclaims: In the mountains, You are there. In the rivers, You are there. In the depths or heights, You are there. In hatred, You are there. In containment, You are there. In love, You are very there. In emptiness, You are there. In loss, You will appear. In horror, I have no one else but You.

Dare I call You Self? You are closer to me than I am, closer than Self. You have made me more caring, more frightened, braver. You who are more, I am more through You.

Contents

Acknowledgments

Many thanks to Dr. George P. Zimmar, director of Psychosocial Press, and Ms. Joanne Freeman, editor, for their prompt and judicious suggestions in readying this book for publication. Thanks also to Mr. Michael Payne Thomas, representing Publisher Charles C Thomas for permitting use of material from "A Flying Phobia: Mind-Body Splits and Individuation," included in Chapter 7 (pp. 133–153) of *Psychoanalysis Today: A Case Book*, edited by Elizabeth Thorne and Shirley Hescovitch Schaye (1991). This material was incorporated in Chapter Two of this volume. My thanks to my wife and children for giving me time to act in timely fashion to Dr. Zimmar's and Ms. Freeman's recommendations.

I am most of all indebted to my patients, Les and Lynn, who gave me chances to use myself and grow in helpful ways. As a therapist, one discovers on a daily basis new turns to the old adage that by helping others one helps oneself.

Reshaping the Self

Les, Lynn, and I are all indebted to the 1960s. Many of us touched by the revolution of lifestyle symbolized by the '60s need to feel our lives have some communal value. The search for workable links between the personal and communal can take many years. This book is a meditation in the '90s on work begun in the '60s. It is meant to help mediate the work of personal-communal renewal in everyday life.

Introduction

What one learns upon opening a body is amazing, but
what one experiences when a psyche begins opening is,
I think, more amazing. Every being channels myriad
worlds. The universe itself, with its endless worlds, seems
an extravagant act of imagination. Imagination may make
us cowards, but it adds drama and color to an experiential flow that is already dramatic and colorful. What makes
life interesting are the links among perception, imagination, and affect. Without this interweaving, life would be
drab. With it, we are rich. As I. B. Singer wrote, "God gave
us so many emotions and such strong ones. Every human
being, even if he is an idiot, is a millionaire in emotions."

Nevertheless, the links between our selves and our
capacities can go awry. Links among perception, imagination, and affect can be wounded, warped, stunted, sev-
ered. Our lives can tick on without us, take wrong turns,
become unrecognizable. We may feel we do not fit our
own body, temperament, character, personality, parents,
social life, or times. We do not fit our selves.

Reshaping the Self

For some individuals, the lack of fit between self and life is not so drastic, but still alarming. There is a nagging sense of something "off." Individuals may seek help in locating what feels wrong. Some need help even to admit that something *is* wrong. They ignore the "something off" signal as long as possible. Some fear that delving into what feels wrong will swallow them up and destroy their lives.

The psychotherapies of Les and Lynn, the focus of this book, teach us that even small changes in one's sense of self can go a long way towards solving problems. Far from experiencing the dreaded destruction, these two patients gained a sense of renewal and redirection. When we are not one with our selves, the lack of fit can be generative. Self tries to reshape self so that interlacings of perception, imagination, and affect work better. However, left to their own devices, Lynn's and Les's lives started to sour. Their attempts to help themselves led to dead ends. Self was spinning wheels rather than reshaping. Lynn and Les needed a professional helping hand to enable intrinsic rhythms and capacities to regroup and find paths that felt right.

My notes on sessions with Lynn and Les date from the 1970s. They are unrelated individuals whom I saw relatively early in my career. I've written about Les twice previously (1981, 1991), although not with the detailed consideration in this volume. I'm drawn to them now because of their relative psychological naiveté and therapeutic purity. They were not chronic cases with long exposure to psychotherapy. They came from outside the therapy field, made use of it, then left to live their lives. This does not sound like much, but long experience teaches me that it is not as usual as one would like. Therapy becomes a way of life for many individuals, often necessarily so. Lynn and Les, in contrast, were able to use therapy to reshape themselves and go on living.

I am also drawn to these two patients because they were children of the 1960s. They came of age on feminist and anti-war protest marches. They were nourished by the Beatles. Their inner beings were stamped with the turmoil and personalist sensibility of the times. Yet life swept them on—into marriage and family, the need to make a living, the need to carve out a decent existence in difficult times. However, the values that marked the '60s continued working in Lynn and Les, even though their lives took fairly traditional shapes. Their problems mirror those experienced by many others of their generation.

By the time I saw them, they were sensing something lacking. Les was a businessman, Lynn a school teacher. Each felt their work fit them. It was not a matter of being in the wrong field. Rather, they needed help in finding ways to do their work so that it could become more congruent with who they felt they were. They needed to find ways to realign themselves with their work so that their basic beliefs and values would be recognizable in what they did. The cutthroat business world and bureaucratic school system mitigated against expression and fulfillment of more personal values. To be oneself and live as one believed meant to go against the grain. The forces against a personal existence one could affirm were enormous.

Les and Lynn also needed help to reconcile the self-other/mind-body currents that would play a role in their growth. We are organized around the double coordinates of self-other and mind-body. Throughout my career, battles have waged as to how best to talk about these terms, which are integral to the discourse of our age. They are part of a struggle to constitute ourselves more fully. We grow through their usage.

For Les and Lynn, the sense of self-other/mind-body had become oppressive, although they could not say so. An unconscious sense of restriction, even suffocation, marred their lives. They could not pinpoint what was wrong. Insofar as they located what was wrong, they could not change it. Heightened states of consciousness that did not get anywhere alternated with helpless oblivion.

The story of therapy is, in part, the story of how the unconscious sense of self-other/mind-body opens. The individual learns to dip in and out of the unconscious more freely and experience the joy that comes with awareness.

I felt honored to be able to contribute to Les's and Lynn's becoming more one with their selves and their directions in life. They were real people working with real problems, both personal and social. Helping them reconnect with their selves and their lives must help the parts of society they affect to become a bit better, too. Instead of being crushed by social pressures, which was indeed a danger when they sought help, each was able to find ways of coping with and contributing to the world. The contribution psychotherapy itself makes to society may be small but, I think, very real.

From time to time over the years, I've met Lynn shopping and see how she has flourished. Her family has grown, and she has had a fine work career. Her life is full, although far from trouble free. She has wrestled with the challenges of her life and functioned as a resource for her students. Les has called me periodically for help with specific problems, but it has been more than a decade since I last heard from him. By now his children are young men and women. When I vacation in New England, I sometimes see ads for his business, which has prospered within the community.

On a personal level, writing this book helps me link up with the therapist me of twenty years ago. My older and newer selves meet in dialogue about self-other and mind-body relations, the dramatic interplay of faith and catastrophe, dream work, and other elements of the psychotherapy process. Lynn's and Les's therapies ended more than fifteen years ago, about halfway through my career. One wonders, for better or worse, how differently things might go now. I'm embarrassed at the crudity of some of my early interventions, but I'm embarrassed about what I do and say now, too. It is also touching to link up with Lynn's and Les's earlier selves. We are middle-aged or older now, but in this volume we are fresh, trying to begin anew.

I've decided to let it all hang out, warts and all. The fact that Lynn and Les really did get better is a tribute to the power of the therapy situation to survive, transcend, absorb, and even use the frailties and warps of those who participate in it, especially those of the practitioner. Once started, there is an objective momentum to therapeutic work that goes beyond the sum of the participants' shortcomings and facilitates the growth process.

What growth processes are and what it means to facilitate them are problematic issues. But we continue to work, and usually some good comes of it. Diverse formulations of so many therapeutic schools bear witness to the elusive quality of the doing. Yet something does happen, and we keep trying to say more about it. Some of what we say helps for a time, but our formulations are often skins that we have already slipped out of.

In the meantime, we continue to grow in the actual doing and happening. At times we seem to speak from the growing itself. The act of growing becomes conscious of itself and finds a momentary expressive language. During these moments, speaking, doing, and being ignite and enrich one another, like sparks dancing across abysses. My writings about my work with Lynn and Les are offered in this open spirit. They stand or fail to the extent they contribute to growth processes not only in Lynn, Les, and myself, but also in the reader.

Chapter One

Bits of the Processing Puzzle

Les and Lynn were hard-working professionals committed to family life. But for each marriage had become a battleground, and the workplace seemed to make integrity impossible. Both individuals felt smothered by the very choices they hoped would fulfill them.

Both Lynn and Les loved their family and professional lives. Marriage and profession made life richer. Yet Lynn and Les twisted themselves out of shape to make things work. Family and professional life exerted pressure on them to live lies and forced them into distortions of self. The institutions that gave them a place and made exercise of their talents possible also poisoned their existence. The constant need to compromise and perform tasks of questionable value eroded their connection with their selves.

When Lynn and Les began their respective therapies, they did not know what was wrong. They just knew something was not working, something was missing. They suffered from a mute sense that life ought to be different. It could not be *this* way. Les used a phobia, fear of flying, as an excuse to get help. At first, Lynn did not know why she came or what sort of help she wanted. She just came.

It did not take long for Les and Lynn to locate many sources of pain and for the stream of suffering to begin flowing. To an extent, therapy moves from pain to pain, from wound to wound. Wounds are like footprints through years, vanishing in points of origin.

Something is Wrong

It takes some individuals years to connect with the sense that something is wrong with their lives. Lynn and Les had many pleasures, many things right with their lives. It was natural to focus on good things and play down bad ones.

Nevertheless, each patient suffered secretly from a sense that things were not as they should be. For many years they kept this sense that something was askew a secret even from themselves. It is not easy to admit something is wrong with one's life. One may feel helpless to do anything about it or fear one will do the wrong things and make the situation worse. It is difficult to listen to the voice of truth that says we have married the wrong person, gone into the wrong profession, settled in the wrong place, become the wrong self.

We get used to ourselves, our routes, our choices. We settle into what is reachable. We may envy what is beyond us, yet make the most of what we have until the voice of truth that eggs us on pushes through years of relative silence and says, "You're living a lie!"

This bring on anxieties about the changes needed. Does one have to get a divorce, change professions, move, get a new self? And if one did, would this solve things or would that nagging feeling continue? Would the still, small voice resurface and haunt us again?

Truth can be tyrannical. The voice of truth can get too demanding and eat up existence like a "Pac Man." Compromise can be corrosive. Even language recognizes this: To be "compromised" refers to loss of integrity. One is caught between truth and compromise. Yet either truth or compromise can be freeing.

This is where therapy comes in. Therapy is a place where one's truths and compromises can have their say. Too often the self is a chorus in which each section goes its own way. The result is cacophony rather than music. Yet each voice has a right to exist and a contribution to make. In therapy each voice gets a maximum say. Truths and compromises can begin to spin dialogical webs.

A context greater than the sum of one's products and positions evolves. Truths and compromises interact in unexpected ways. One finds the expanding, interactive field more interesting than being an advocate for a set position. One discovers one does not have to be dominated by truth or collapsed by compromise. One is more than the sum of one's truths and compromises.

Les's Background

It is odd but fitting to say that one can be bigger or smaller than one's life. We hint at this when we say that someone is larger than life. Sometimes we are smaller, sometimes bigger, depending on mood, attitude, circumstances, rhythm. Les never quite felt the right size. He was either too big or too small for himself and his existence.

At times Les and his life came together. It was exhilarating for him to cut a good business deal. During some moments at home with his family his heart filled to bursting. Nevertheless, he felt a nagging sense that he was not getting it right, that he was living the wrong life—or the right life the wrong way. Something noxious would grow in the middle of a wonderful feeling, spoiling the best that he could do.

He imagined buying a camper and taking off. He would start over, leave everything behind, become pure again. Sometimes he imagined taking his family with him. They would live in the woods, far from pressures that warped him. He would experience real difficulties working with nature, not the phony challenges of climbing the corporate ladder.

The truth is that Les loved business and was good at it. But he felt twisted out of shape working in a big company. He hated being subservient to bosses, overbearing to subordinates, manipulative with both. He hated himself for playing the game. Yet he didn't know what else he could do, or ought to do. He was being poisoned by what he liked doing best.

The twisted feeling gnawed at him. His mother always wanted him to be a big man in a big company. He fulfilled her desire. Indeed, he *was* her desire. She empowered him. Her faith in him made him successful.

She was in back of him, if he lived life on her terms. And for most of his life, his and her terms had been one.

Still, his feelings of rebellion led to her. He might be grateful that she enabled him to develop his abilities, yet something was "off" at the core of his identity. She was at the center of his being, at the very place where he should be. Nothing he did felt right because it was not he doing it. She stained his achievements.

Does the knight win everything for mother? Les's innermost feelings said no. Les was fighting for himself, for his *own* life. He enjoyed the prizes he won, even if tainted. To win one's own life—is this possible? It was interesting to speculate what a better fit between Les and his life would be like. Or was it naive to think there *could* be a better fit? Isn't identity always stained by otherness?

There is freeing as well as stifling otherness. Les never felt so free than at certain moments with Terry, his wife and friend. There were times with Terry when just walking down a street made Les feel, "This is the way life ought to be." The problem was that they fought most of the time. To an extent, battle is part of freedom. But they wore each other down, made life impossible. Still, Terry saved Les from himself. She did not seem to live someone else's life. She was simply herself. Her spontaneous presence made Les feel that real living was possible. However, all paths he tried were blocked. If Terry had been enough, Les would not have had to seek therapy.

Les was most deeply moved by his children. But the freedom and happy times he enjoyed with them were eroded by worry. The idea that they might die, be kidnapped, or come into harm's way was terrifying. Dread of catastrophe gave Les no rest. It spoiled his happiest moments.

You might think any of the above—twisted self, hated job, domineering mother, marital discord, terror of catastrophe—could be enough to send Les into therapy. But Les could only let himself seek help for a more circumscribed problem: fear of flying. Here was something he could give to the therapist without risking too much. He could bring a specific symptom, a little bit of himself. If *it* changed, his life could go on along the same lines, business as usual. He could hide behind and bring *it*, instead of *himself*.

It is easier to seek help if we lie a little. Les could not come in and say, "Here I am, a mess. I'm a wreck and my life is awful. I don't know what went wrong." He was used to seeing himself as a big man, someone of importance, a winner. He was high on the corporate ladder, a contributing member of his community, a visible person. He was a good family man, a man who cared. It was tactful of his psyche to give him an excuse, a reason removed enough from his closest self, something "out there" to fix.

What surprised both of us was how quickly his closest self came out. Les had a therapy hunger. It was as if he had been secretly waiting years for the chance to spill, to speak himself out, to cry from the heart. In truth, the "off point" of his life tortured him. A corner of his inner eye never left the lie he lived. It was as if a barium tracer lit up the poison that ran through him; he never dared to look at it directly, nor could he look away.

Lynn's Background

Lynn, like Les, struck me as a tense person. She was not driven to make big money, but she took pride in her work and strove to do the best she could. Lynn was an art and photography teacher in high school, and was especially dedicated to photography. Being a creative teacher was a constant struggle. The "system" wore her down. She battled not only the inertia and hostility of students but also the crassness and lack of interest of school administrators, who were preoccupied with salary increments and management problems. She persistently had to distort herself and go against enormous pressures to make room for what she wanted to do. Within the system, there were networks of dedicated people who drew strength from one another, although not enough to offset the strain they were under.

Lynn looked to her marriage for nourishment, only to discover new sets of problems. She and her husband jockeyed for position. Their differing tempos and rhythms created friction, and they irritated each other. Although they loved each other, they did not know what to do with each other. Home was supposed to be a haven, and to an extent it was. But it also was a source of strain and tension. Neither Lynn nor her husband wanted to live alone or without each other, yet life together seemed a parade of disturbances.

The odd thing was that deep down they felt united and connected. Theirs was a subterranean oneness, as if deep under the surface their roots intertwined. They fit each other somewhere out of view on an unconscious

7

intercellular or soul level. But on earth's surface they annoyed each other, and ego clashed against ego. The separation above was not in sync with the oneness below.

Whichever way Lynn turned, life was a battle. She was close to her family, her parents, brother and sister. She was involved with them, and they with her. Yet they drove her to distraction and, in varying ways, infuriated her. Each relationship was a love-hate struggle. Her relationships with friends offered some solace and relief. But she and they also pulled the rug out from under one another. It was as if relationships had to be tested and challenged. If a relationship survived difficulties, it must be worth something; it must be real.

Lynn oscillated between being pinched and full, between strain and pleasure. A certain tightness rarely left her. To an extent, she thrived on pressure. However, she was also misshapen by the very pressure she needed. I felt that she made herself less than she could be, that she was constantly straining against inner-outer forces and boundaries that constricted her.

Lynn did not offer any reason or excuse for seeking therapy. Nor did she seem to reach out for help, at least not at the beginning. Perhaps she just sought a place that was different, a place outside the system of strains, where she could just wait and be.

Different Approaches to Therapy

Les was propelled into therapy by unsettling fears and terrors. Lynn found herself coming without any clear reason or justification. They were "ordinary" people caught in the treadmill of work and daily chores. They were not "therapy types." Therapy was not something they sought whenever things went wrong or something they would hold on to for many, many years.

Yet they were not totally naive about therapy. They had ideas about what therapy was like, or should be like. They were educated, verbal, active people. At the outset, both dominated sessions with verbal outpourings. In time, they were to take very different directions in therapy. Each sought or created different core experiences. Each made of therapy a very different journey.

Both Lynn and Les had sparkle and élan. They were alive, busy people who looked as if they were capable of enjoying themselves. They expected to be appreciated, to be celebrated. For Les and Lynn, life was enlivening. They were very different from patients who come in collapsed and lifeless, crushed by events, lost in meaninglessness. Lynn and Les were not dead or lost. They were not done in by life.

In a mirror, they could recognize themselves and like what they saw. But they also might see tense and nervous versions of themselves, distortions of themselves. Les was normally jumpier than Lynn. He was used to anxiety streaming through his body, driving him to action. Lynn sat on it more. To an extent, both Lynn and Les were twisted out of shape by anxiety into caricatures of themselves.

Les and Lynn were both used to living with a high degree of tension. In some measure, tension fueled their lives. Their existences would have felt strange and empty without a lot of tension. In addition, both were used to and needed a high level of activity. The paradox was that although Lynn and Les thrived on tension and a high activity, there were ways in which their personalities could not keep up with the tensions they generated.

Their personalities courted and engendered more tension than they could handle. Personality changes evolve with tension levels. In certain situations we tense up. Physical muscles tighten in characteristic patterns. Psychological muscles tighten, too. Expressive features and self-feelings change together. Personalities get distorted, explosive, fusional. We are not the selves we want to be. We are afraid of ourselves, sit on ourselves, hide, feel unable to handle the flood or face the barrier.

Les was used to acting like a big businessman. He filled the therapy space with self-importance. He dictated the order of the day, set the agenda. Therapy would be about what he wanted. He treated therapy like a business deal. It was a matter of finding the right combination of factors to achieve the desired results. Something was wrong; find out what and fix it. Les took for granted an ideology of mastery.

If a car does not work, a mechanic makes necessary repairs. Similarly, a surgeon cleans tubes, splices channels, removes offending material. Les's manner was brisk, hurried. He did not have time for hemming and hawing, sloppiness, uncertainty. He believed that we are creative, goal-oriented machines, captains of our fate. The idea that we are also mysteries was terrifying to him.

Les expected me to be the captain of the therapy ship. He knew what he was doing in his business. I ought to know what to do in mine. The idea that growth demanded openness, time, evolution bothered him. He wanted control. The tone and pace of therapy was slower and less cluttered than daily life in business. Les regarded my pace as slow motion, my calm deathlike. I had more questions than answers. In fact, I had no answers at all, and scarcely any suggestions. My office was another planet.

In therapy our worlds clashed—two different temperaments, two sets of rhythms, two mindsets. Les tried to quicken the pace, create an aura of control, stimulate hysteria, while I tinkered with reality, offered background support, and questioned assumptions. The battle between openness and control was on.

Lynn also was active, verbal, and controlling but felt that she lost something in the struggle for control. She was more aware than Les of liabilities attached to an ideology of mastery and control. Whether she won or lost a battle, she lost herself. She became keenly aware of how she tightened and stiffened in the fight to win. She was good at having her say and not backing down, but the price was chronic and great. She asserted herself but lost fullness of being.

It was important that Lynn stick up for herself. She had to fight for what she believed in at the workplace and at home. She would be less a person if she did not. Nevertheless, the importance of fighting stole Lynn from herself. If she did not fight, she lost herself. However, in fighting she lost herself also. She became a smaller, more brittle version of herself. She could feel a smallness in her pinched face, tightness between shoulders, stiffening of lower back. She tightly held on to herself and was terrified of opening. She was used to holding herself in without quite realizing that she was squeezing herself.

Lynn was used to asserting herself and did not know what to do with the sense that she held herself back. She felt the strain of gearing for battle. Her voice sounded metallic. She would get a variety of physical symptoms, aches, and pains. Her way of solving problems was more self-assertive, more tightening, more pushing. She could feel her body and insides contracting, but she did not know what to do.

Lynn wanted to contact herself at a deeper level. Whereas Les wanted feelings in order to master them, Lynn simply wanted them. She wanted to feel feelings, to feel herself. She did not want to go through life missing herself. Les was so filled with himself it scarcely occurred to him that *he* might be missing. Perhaps he went about things the wrong way, perhaps there was something he could do to correct what he did. For Lynn the issue became whether or not she could dip into being and how much of it she could tolerate.

Action was important to Lynn. She was never a person to sit around. She fought injustices in marriage and at school. She fought inequities in the system. She could not be a doormat or loser. Battle was endless. Momentary successes were followed by more abuse in need of correction. The jungle grew faster than it could be cleared. She could not give up. And there *were* satisfactions.

Lynn felt in danger of being consumed by her fight for good against bad. Her fighting spirit was so pervasive (and she always felt in the right) that no particle of her life seemed exempt from it. Through fighting, she grew in a specialized way but also felt more and more a sliver of herself. Lynn was so used to fighting for her rights that she did not know when she was fighting. The fighting continued when she was alone, permeating her being. Lynn grew used to fighting herself without realizing it. She was not in danger of breaking down or collapsing into inertia, but she was in danger of failing to become a good friend to herself, a good partner to her life. Lynn feared that she would fight her way through life and come up empty. She would fight on the side of life, but miss real living. Lynn, to an extent, used therapy as a place where she could drop below her fight with the world and her fight with herself, and search for the sabbath point of her soul.

Society and Self

Defining relationships between society and self is a never-ending problem. There are viewpoints that say self transcends society or that different aspects of society reflect different aspects of self. Other viewpoints trace social and cultural factors in the constitution of the self. Increasingly, we emphasize reciprocal relationships between self and society. We learn about society by studying self and learn about self by studying society.

The many ideologies that claim knowledge about self and society often clash with one another. We do not know very much about mediating competing claims. We hope that plurality of voices does not become babble, and that mutual impact means mutual fertilization.

We speak, hoping we have something to say. Yet centuries of self-criticism teach us that communication is permeated with self-deception and self-interest. We speak in the service of images. There are always hidden subtexts. We are like centipedes counting legs, spotting lies as fast as words come out. Some of us are silenced by the vision of complexity, while some of us wink and try to cut a slice of a winning lie.

We lust for truth but can't be fanatic about it. We know whatever we come up with, whatever speaks through us, must be fragmentary, a bit of evolution. This does not detract from the suffering and joy of farming a piece of what we are given, our arena of discovery.

I do not have the illusion that what I do will change society much, if at all, although it may have some impact on societal subgroups. I am not a social reformer, much as I might like to be. My vocation is working with individuals. In some ways, I am an individual reformer, or at least striving to provide a context where individuals can reformulate themselves. I would like to think that if an individual life becomes a little better, the world becomes a little better. However, my experience of the world has not given me the right to think this.

Experience teaches me that individuals *can* change for the better. This does not mean that problems go away, that suffering ends, that one becomes an entirely new person. I doubt that anyone becomes the kind of person they would like to be. Nevertheless, it *is* possible to form better links with oneself, to shift the tone of one's relationship with oneself, to develop a different qualitative "feel" for what one is up against.

The change I have in mind is, in part, atmospheric or textural. The individual "vibes" differently, resonates differently. No one can take or process the full dose of pain that comes one's way, any more than one can experience a total dose of God without filters. But a context develops that better cushions, absorbs, and processes bits of experience. One does life more justice.

It is interesting to consider whether an individual can be helped if the social context remains the same. What sense does it make to cure individuals if society is incurable? The terms of such statements are dizzying. Individuals are incurable, too, and society keeps changing. Many pockets of society offer us more than we can use, while other aspects of society warp us. We do not have a clear, indisputable picture of what change and constancy mean. We do not know how best to work with ourselves and our products. We try this and that and see what happens.

Lynn never overcame the warp in the system. It ran through her personality. To an extent, she remained reactive to a twist she could not cure. Nevertheless, she grew, thawed out, opened. Her relationship to the warp deepened. She became more responsive to herself. Her fighting was not merely alienating. Life had more volume and color, even if she were never free of difficulties.

Lynn was as incurable as the system. Lynn's and the system's intractability fit together, although no one-to-one correlation existed between them. The boundaries of the intractable can shift, but warp, deficit, paralysis, and numbness can never entirely be outgrown or wished away. One's relationship to the intractable merely deepens. To some extent, the intractable forces us to pull back and leap farther, to use more might and cunning, to exercise our selves in new ways. Our dialogue with limits (our own, the world's, those of change or constancy) is part of what brings us closer to ourselves and one another. Struggle with boundaries is part of what makes partnership with our capacities possible.

Les did not change the system so much as shift the direction of his thrust. Lynn remained a teacher, and Les a businessman. Both continued to do what they liked and did best, what they felt fit them. Les found a way to matter more, first of all, to himself. He wanted to work and play hard, but not in cutthroat fashion. He needed to reconnect with himself and his work so that he would not feel lost or crowded. He explored the possibility of developing a genuinely personal approach to business instead of a kill-or-be-killed outlook. He sought ways both to be a businessman and to maintain integrity, rather than tolerate erosion of integrity as a matter of course. Les's therapy became a probing ground for those issues in which the quality of his life was at stake.

In exploring individuals, therapy explores warps, poisons, and ills in society. Therapy sessions are microcosms of social ills. One may cynically observe that therapy is part of the illness, that cure is another form of disease. Who would argue? Yet my brain and heart tell me that Lynn and Les were better off because of therapy. Lynn opened up. Les redirected the course of his life. For both Les and Lynn, quality of life changed for the better. Both made more use of their selves, more use of others. A palpable, tonal shift occurred in their relationship to the universe. When compared to the vast sea of social ills, such changes are microscopic. In the lives of individuals, such changes are as miraculous as the parting of seas.

Processing Experience

Lynn and Les had plenty of experience. The problem was in the way they processed, or failed to process, this experience. Their lives brimmed over with events and emotions, but the feeling of being incomplete did not go away. Activity, hysteria, fighting, and panic did not drown it out for long. The "off feeling" or "off point" threatened to spoil whatever good happened.

The "off point" was not being processed. Lynn and Les had plenty of ideas about their lives. They mulled over events and feelings and put together narrative versions of their histories. They could relate what was wrong to aspects of parenting and society. Yet they were hemmed in by their versions of themselves. The "thing that was off" did not budge.

The "off point" never goes away. Human beings have been talking about it for thousands of years. Sin, madness, folly, pride are some of the terms that have been used in this discourse. In recent years, social-economic inequity has been the ideological frontrunner for deciphering the sense that something is wrong. One cannot stop the rush of reality. Ideologies clash. People clash. There are fights over territory, boundaries of every sort: among nations, races, genders, classes, generations, siblings.

Psychoanalysis and literature are obsessed with the ways people destroy themselves by the manner in which they choose (or are driven) to *be* themselves. It is not simply a matter of to be or not to be. One may be conflicted about alternate ways of being and alternate sets of identities. The system may wear or break one down. But one can also be broken by one's identity.

Every identity has a downside, opens and closes possibilities, enhances and detracts from existence. Some individuals do a better job than others at juggling identities. One has to be concerned not only with the fit between sets of identities and the slices of society one moves in but also with the fit between one's alternate identities and one's self. One may never feel comfortable with one's dominant identities. To invest in an identity that is wrong for one can be disastrous. One may be inextricably wedded to an identity that is suffocating or leads one down a path one knows is wrong. One clings to this fallacious identity as it takes one over the brink, even as one sinks. An individual can drown in his or her identity.

Lynn and Les sought help with what was in danger of turning into the long suicide of their lives. They were slowly and pleasurably being eaten up by the sorts of persons they had become. Without quite realizing it, their identities became cloying, bothersome, got in the way. They were a muddled blend of right and wrong identities— right and wrong persons living in a right and wrong world.

Les and Lynn needed to process the sort of persons they had become, as well as the sort of world they lived in. They took their basic identity feelings for granted, even when these feelings struck them as wrong. Identity

18

feelings are part of our personal environment. They facilitate or hinder personal movement. Some aspects of identity help move our lives forward, while other aspects block or even sabotage personality growth.

There are times when growth of personal being gets ahead of the identity feelings we are used to. At such moments we may stand between identity systems and taste an exquisite sense of freedom. It can be terrifying to confuse our selves with a crumbling sense of identity, but joyously liberating to discover that we outlast our identities. We come through our selves and our identities. We catch on that life involves lagging behind and outstripping our selves, that something deep and wonderful beyond categories evolves.

Les and Lynn substituted their sense of identity for a more open relationship to experiencing. Perhaps this is one reason that Lynn was bored with herself and that Les felt caught in vicious spirals. They were stuck on smaller versions of their selves and went round and round the same fights and frustrations. The flow of experience was funneled through identity systems that churned out well-worn scenarios. Les and Lynn became automatic versions of themselves. Both wanted to live more fully but were trapped by their identities. They were squeezed too tightly into their versions of themselves. They came to therapy, in part, because their lives did not fit them, and they did not fit their selves.

In retrospect, I wonder if the processing task wasn't easier for Les than for Lynn. Things seemed clearer for him. Not only could he locate what he hated in the external world, it was also obvious that his mother was a part of what he hated in his world. She dominated him and forced him to conform. It was not too difficult to locate the inner-outer tyrants that needed to be faced. It was more a matter of going on the journey, joining the battle. With help, Les gradually found resources to pinpoint and work with sources of self-betrayal.

Lynn's difficulties, at first, were more nebulous, less focused. As her therapy evolved, she seemed to be searching for missing capacities, missing experiences. Her relationships with the outer world certainly changed. But in Lynn's case, the processing path was more circuitous, more involved with sensed nuances of feeling.

Furthermore, Lynn had to battle with apparently betraying her earlier feminist ideology, or adapting it to what really mattered to her. Her inner search led to the intimation that what she most wanted was children and a viable family life. This took precedence over professional ambition. At the same time, she did not want to be tyrannized by her need for family. She needed her relationships with her husband, her work, herself, and her potential children to evolve. She did not give up working and struggled to find ways to make her work the worthwhile humanistic activity she envisioned. She searched for ways to integrate all elements of her life into a profoundly personal existence capable of satisfactory growth.

Pulsations

In the chapters ahead, I describe some of the processes that made a difference in Lynn's and Les's lives. It may turn out that I did injustice to a most important element since it is almost impossible to describe with any accuracy the therapy atmosphere—the tone or spirit of communication that existed over long periods of time.

Here two of us were, in a room together, one to three times a week for five or so years. I liked Lynn and Les, perhaps loved them in ways. My feelings toward them kept changing. They intimidated me, they warmed me, they irritated me, they alarmed me. I felt joy in sharing the unfolding of their lives. I felt frustrated, defeated, saddened over how difficult and limited growth processes are. My heart and mind opened and closed in myriad ways. I felt nuances of despair and experienced moments of cautious hope. At times I got out of the way. A hidden range-finder and processor really worked. I had to stretch to let Lynn's and Les's impacts play on me so that bits of impacts grew into usable responses.

I was sorry to see each of them go. I wished I could have done better. But I knew I had done the best I could. Out of messy work in trenches, Lynn's and Les's processing ability grew. Therapy provided an arena in which they could exercise their processing ability and reshape their selves. They were able to become more faithful to experience, to let moments evolve, to let their lives expand. They were able to take their next steps.

So much gets left out of case reports: casual jokes, passing words of encouragement, gestures of exasperation, smiles, twinkling eyes, eyes closing as one fearfully or happily dozes off, a mixture of reliability and unpredictability, changing blends of security and stimulation, worry, everydayness, ecstasy.

Is it possible to catch primary process in the act? Is the self ever completely naked? There is always some disguise. Yet something comes through in the act of writing. Writing is not simply retelling. It is also a wrestling with the affective impact of therapy—not just in the moment but in the aftermath of the moment, replete with the shock waves. I took notes for these chapters nearly verbatim during the sessions themselves. But I did not know beforehand how they would organize themselves in the writing.

In the succeeding chapters, we see how Lynn and Les became tangled in their young lives. They had made good starts that they felt stuck with even though their lives had become oppressive, not only because of circumstances but also because of their own personalities. Open doors they had gone through seemed to shut behind them. They were driven into therapy in search of an opening. All other avenues had ended in walls. Perhaps therapy merely provides another set of walls, a repatterning of walls. Yet I feel that there are openings. We move from wall to wall, from opening to opening.

Lynn's and Les's therapies are still alive for me. By letting their sessions speak through me now, I learn more about what happened years ago and grow through this contact. Writing about therapy stimulates growth of therapeutic capacity. The affective resonance of sessions produces new waves of insight, a bit like light pulsations from distant stars. The stars lie deep within, and the pulsations bring one to new places.

Chapter Two

Defining Moments in Les's Therapy

Big Man

Les announced when he began therapy that he wanted help because he was a successful coordinator of sales for a big business firm and was afraid of flying. His fear of flying prevented him from pursuing higher positions in his company and made his present position painful. He flew when he had to, but the personal cost in coping with panic was high. He went through elaborate machinations to find ways of avoiding trips or to invent excuses for going by car.

My inclination was to point out the ambiguous note sounded in his presenting complaint. "Are you saying you want help because you are the successful coordinator of sales for a big business firm or because you are afraid of flying or both?"

Les bragged about his success: he had come so far; he could go further. After he felt he had painted a suc-cessful enough picture, he owned that he loved sales and business but hated the fear and kowtowing that seemed to be part of dealing with bosses and competitors. He hated the corporate structure.

"Maybe your fear of flying is a protest. Maybe it has a wisdom. Have you ever felt like throwing the whole thing over?"

"God yes. But I have a family, kids, a life."

He told me more about how successful he was and everything that depended on it. He needed to show me what a big man he was before he could let down a little more. Before the session ended, I asked if he would be happy if I could fix his fear of flying so he could continue rising on the corporate ladder. Was that all he needed?

"I love my wife and kids," he pleaded. "But Terry and I fight like cats and dogs. We have great sex. We're great on vacations. When we leave the kids and go off to Cape Cod we're terrific. The rest of the time we kill each other."

"That's it?"

"I'm terrified for my kids. I have awful nightmares. They get stolen or killed. I live in terror."

From bravado to terror. Not bad for a first session with a big man. I wondered how long he would stay with me and how far we could go. To my surprise, Les worked hard with me for five years and might have continued longer if the main change he unconsciously sought had not occurred.

The Setting

In the first months of therapy, Les went over the story of his life. Telling his story brought some relief but also was scary because of challenges it set.

Defining Moments in Les's Therapy

His mother was the driving force in his family throughout his childhood and adult life. She was a political force in his hometown and expected big things of her sons.

Les felt he disappointed her. Nothing he did was good enough. Since he was a little boy he had tried to reach for more than he could handle and became adept at trying. He put everything into whatever he did and could be counted on for all-out effort. Even if Les fell short of goals he or his mother set, he developed many skills along the way. He became likable and got along with people.

When it came time for college Les wanted to stay home and go to a local school, but his mother pushed him to go away to a big university. He obediently did his best but became uncontrollably nervous. The counselor at school could not help. In a fit of panic he returned home and weathered his mother's scorn, which was milder than he had expected. Although he disappointed her, she seemed relieved to have him back. He did well commuting to business school.

After school he started a small business with his brother Stan. Les remembered the two years that he worked at his store as the best he ever had. The idea that the store was his thrilled him. He felt at the center of things. When things went poorly, he did not want to sell out but gave in to his mother's and brother's pressure. Afterwards he was haunted by the sense that he might have made a go of it if he had withstood his mother's protestations. He hated himself for not going it alone. The rub was that at heart he was sheepish and slavish and knew it.

Les's mother felt her sons should make it with a big corporation and in politics. A small store in a small town seemed wasteful and silly. Yet she insisted that Les and his brother devote themselves to community tasks, and they worked hard and well in her election campaigns. She never lost an election, and in their small town they would always be Bess's sons.

A Family of His Own

Les married Terry, who liked the good life but was very naturally her own person. She and Les fought a lot. Her moods expressed a discontent that was part of the family atmosphere.

They married when he was in business school, soon after his collapse at college. She soothed and supported him and provided the sexual incentive to make him feel that life was worthwhile and that he was a worthwhile person. She stood by him in his business and nursed him through its failure.

Terry felt something was wrong but did not pinpoint Bess, at least not for a long time and then not sharply. She did her best to get along from day to day, taking care of house and children, finding part-time work she enjoyed. Bess liked Terry, perhaps because she was a local girl who had no urge to move away. Les's marriage meant he would never be far from her.

Terry was easygoing and sociable. Perhaps Bess mistook her friendliness for compliance and suppressed an inkling that Terry's naturalness presupposed very real autonomy. However, as years wore on Terry proved anything but compliant.

It was, in part, Terry's instinct to be her own person that made Les proud of her. When they fought each other, Les, of course, felt he was right and she wrong. At those moments they hated each other. But he also felt deep down that she was fighting for something more than he was—that she was right about something at bottom. She was fighting for the family as a whole, for all of them. Her refusal or inability to give up her autonomy kept the family alive. Terry was evidence that Les did not marry and stay in his hometown just to please his mother. His family was no mere offering to Bess. His fights with Terry meant he had something of his own.

The Crisis

Les threw himself into therapy with determination and fervor, as he did with all his projects. "Tell me what steps I can take," he often said.

"See what you feel during the week," I might say, leaving things open.

Les would see what he felt with a vengeance. He bought a tape recorder to free-associate into between sessions and kept a dream book. He treated problems as things out there he could attack. It never occurred to him that *he* might be part of the problem.

It did not take Les long to start coming late to sessions, miss sessions, and voice annoyance with therapy. He quickly rediscovered something he long knew and denied. He could not control the psyche or will fears away. His problems did not yield like a business deal. Being a "good boy" or "slave driver" or "expert" tightened knots that bound him.

Yet his efforts had a priming effect. After two years of work, Les's sessions became more feverish. He sensed that alternation of obedience and rebellion marked a larger pattern. Issues of slavery and freedom ran deep. The sores he picked at began to open. The sessions recounted in this chapter marked the onset of a two-year crisis period, which culminated in the decision Les needed to make.

No To Mom: Happiness and Terror

One mid-December day, more than two years after therapy began, Les entered flushed with pride but also worried. He had taken the strongest stand vis-à-vis his mother that he dared.

> Les: "I've told her over and over not to buy me tickets for her functions. She did it again. She bought tickets for a Girl Scout function and wanted me to go with her. I said no. I stopped myself from crying out, 'Yes, I'll go. Don't worry.' I was so busy holding myself back, but I was happy as a little kid. I told her I wanted to be treated as an adult.
>
> "When I told my tape recorder about it, I pictured mother vomiting. My saying no made her sick. My brother would have gone. I felt the pull. I should have gone. A Girl Scout function. It was harmless enough.

Defining Moments in Les's Therapy

"My dreams were horrible. Getting rid of dead bodies. I lost my kids. Violence. In the morning my happy feeling was almost gone. I felt guilty. When I told my wife about the phone call, she said, 'I hope you didn't hurt her.' I wanted to call my mother and ask about her cold. 'No, Les,' I told myself. 'Don't call her and apologize. Guilty feelings will leave.' They did by three o'clock. It was O.K. I could still feel the happiness.

"She [mother] called at three and said she felt there was more I wanted to say. Can you believe the timing? The moment I felt good again she called. She said she waited to see if I would call. She spoke to Terry. She wanted Terry to tell me I was wrong. Terry didn't want me to hurt her but knew I felt strongly.

"I held on to my strength. She [mother] didn't want to be wrong. She sounded as if she would cry and said she didn't want to lose rapport with me.

"She was always proud of the great communication we had. I was, too. From the earliest age I felt we were very close. We understood each other. We had a special warmth. She didn't have this with my brother or father. She felt I understood her in a way no one else did. It was really beautiful. No rough edges.

"Only now do I begin to see that I fit in with her more than the others. I'd do anything if she liked me. My brother was rougher, more a bully. He had a mean streak. I was nicer. He might finally do what she wanted; look at his way of life. But he had more rough edges. He fought more. She could idealize me more. She could think of me as the good one, the boy of her dreams. She could feel closer to me because I was more compliant. I really wanted to make her happy. Now I begin to see what she called rapport and communication was a kind of blind fusion. Perhaps it was not only that. But did she really know who I was? Look what happens when I say no.

29

"I don't really understand how we could have such a feeling of rapport and closeness and communication when there was so much violence. Once when Stan and I were cutting up she took us for a long car ride, then put us out of the car and drove away. I screamed. My brother didn't care, or so he acted. I was terrified and screamed and screamed. She just drove around the block or so, but it felt forever. I was four or five. What did we do so wrong to get such a horrible punishment? We were probably not listening to her about something. I have the feeling she threatened us with abandonment more than once. Was it a pattern? I was scared to death. How could I be so terrified and feel so close to her? Did I push my rage away to make sure nothing bad would happen to me? To make sure her goodness would shine on me?

"Can you believe she never mentioned the incident again? A few years later I almost didn't believe it happened and asked her, 'Why, Mommy?' She made believe she didn't know what I was talking about. 'You two rascals. You're a much better boy now, don't you think?' She washed my feelings away. I was wrong, she was right. Only the warmth we felt was important.

"My sticking to my no this weekend made her cry. Now she's the abandoned child. This was the first time I can remember talking to her about a feeling and not letting myself be told the feeling was wrong. I just said what I needed to say and stood by it. Whenever I argue she wins. This time my strength shook her.

"I've been feeling more relaxed, the most relaxed I've ever been. I can feel the out and in of my breath. I think I only breathed in before. Now I'm tingling all over. I can relax myself by breathing.

"Terry and I argued over the weekend but weren't unhappy. I enjoy living with Terry most of the time. She doesn't understand therapy. We've gotten closer over the last year or so. I was getting down on our marriage before and I think she was, too. I still don't know which way to go, but we have a lot of good times together. I haven't been depressed for ten days. I kept my happiness alive by not taking those tickets Mom got for me. Our arguments would have been enough to ruin the weekend, but this time a good feeling kept right on going."

I said little as Les was moving nicely. I took the abandonment incident he recounted as paradigmatic of a traumatic element that may have permeated his childhood. His mother may have used separation as a threat in many ways. When he said no to mother, his psyche began to fall apart. His dreams were filled with loss, violence and fragility. However, he weathered the temporary breakdown. Perhaps he feared that he killed his mother or she him. Perhaps he dreaded losing the special bond between them. Her joking and cajoling her way out of Les's accusations set the tone for Les's joking himself out of his own reality as an adult. His standing up to his mother marked the beginning of standing up to himself. He got a taste of coming through disorganizing moments linked with growth processes, a thrilling step which set the tone for things to come.

Dialogue with a Guide

Les's next dreams depicted him in the midst of heroic struggle.

Les: "A group of people stood by the Finger Lakes. The guide and I were getting ready to go on a boat. We had to go through a small body of water to pick up other people. The water was calm like glass, but unpredictable. It becomes extremely violent, waves slashing. We're scared, afraid of going through this, but we have to go through it. Then the body of water becomes still again. A person on a canoe comes down it. The water is still for him but rough for us. We push ahead and get into calm water but the boat now is covered with very poisonous snakes. We have to kill them all, thousands of them. They're small. We can step on them to squash them. We have to be quick to make sure we get them and they don't get us. We wear high boots and are quick. We cleanse the ship.

"Finally we tell people to come aboard. My friend Jack is taking a shower in the kitchen. I see a snake under the table. I look at him [the snake] and he looks at me. My wife's younger sister is taking a shower. A lot of faces are peering, people I know. It's almost like a party for me."

M.E.: "You certainly came through something. Can you talk about it?" [My tone mirrored Les's intensity in telling his dream. That something feels significant is often as important as what significance one makes of it.]

Les: "I came through to peace. The canoe man was my model. That must be you or something growing in me. A human being who has been through it, who knows how to do it now. In the ship I'm learning to work with impulses instead of shutting stuff out. I couldn't do it alone. Killing snakes—that's what had to be done and I was going to do it. At the end everyone reunites. We celebrate. I don't think the shower is sexual."

Defining Moments in Les's Therapy

M.E.: "Part of the cleansing?"

Les: "I'm happy about coming through something, not shutting everything out."

M.E.: "Do you and the guide have more to say to each other?"

Les: "I can hear the guide talking inside me. I say, 'I don't want to do this thing. I'm scared. I don't think I can.'
"He says, 'You have to. It's O.K. I've done it before. We can do it, too, even in rough water.'
"I say, 'I'm just going to stay here.'
"The guide says, 'O.K. You stay, we'll go with the other people.'
"I say, 'I don't want to stay here alone. Which way are we going to go? I'm scared but I'll go.'
"I'm not so afraid once we start. Once I get on the boat I feel strong and secure. I'm active, helping with sailing, going through the dangers. It seems smooth even though it's rough on the banks. We're coming out of it in beautiful, calm, deep water. Now it's happy. Then the guide says, 'There are snakes on the boat. It happens every time we go through water.'
"I'm frightened for my life and say, 'Why didn't you tell me!'
"The guide says, 'You can do it. You must get the right approach. Going through the water is useless if you can't do this. You have to do it all. You can do it.'
"I'm afraid, but as I start stepping on them I find I can do it. I'm in a frenzy killing them, but there's no mess. They disappear. As I kill them the ship gets purified. We yell, 'All aboard.' I'm not sure people want to come on. I'm almost enjoying the rough water and snake

killing. People come aboard. The guide's gone. We're happy and having a good time.

"Maybe the sea is my emotions. The fear I have is the fear to really experience my emotions unless I know they can be controlled. The guide is you but also my mind taking care of the situation, a kind of intelligence that sees through the situation and keeps a proper balance.

"All the people were faceless at first. They did not want to come on board and face the dangers. They cover up feelings like I do. We're so afraid of true emotions, so afraid of losing control. It's safer to be faceless."

Les idealizes analysis (the guide, the canoe man model) and himself. Perhaps he feels he can control the need to control. A tinge of grandiosity characterizes the fearful, heroic snake-killer. Perhaps the big man stance is one of the snakes that multiplies. Do we know what the snakes really mean? Ought he simply to kill them? They may have much to contribute to experiencing, if they can be experienced. Les shows real wisdom when he speaks of an intelligence working in dangerous situations. He is closer to facing dangers with another person, rather than thinking he must solve his problems himself, although the latter view tortures him. More important than any particular interpretation of the dream is the experience of meeting and coming through terrifying dangers. Therapy helps the self come through horrors in ways that are not mainly seductive or manipulative. A shift in the quality of one's style of "coming through" may be the main benefit of psychoanalytic work.

Tug of War

Les came late for the next sessions and demanded I analyze why. I felt he wanted me to apologize for his tardiness, as if it were my fault. He let loose a tirade against analysis. Analysis was a questionable enterprise. He would be a fool not to attack it.

> Les: "I was late on purpose. Something in me goes, 'Heh, heh. I'll show him. I'll get the bastard. He's not going to get me.' My wife's always late and I'm punctual. Others are late but not me. I don't want to behave the way I'm supposed to. You're the professional, what do you say?"

There were problems with last session but I thought it marked a breakthrough. Les did not like the idea of getting help from someone and was scared that I knew more about him than he did; it is difficult not to attribute more knowledge to the analyst than he really has. Analytic success meant there existed uncanny powers of intersubjectivity that Les could not control. The idea of mind meeting mind was frightening. Would I seduce and control and manipulate him like his mother? Fail him like his father? At the same time he reached moments of destiny, points of no return, which produced overload and a need to break away. A Huck Finn, sticking-out-tongue stance preserved freedom and saved him from therapeutic slavery.

> M.E.: "Maybe you came late so you won't have to feel sorry for yourself." [What an odd thing to say. I could

scarcely believe I said it. Damn it! I was being defensive! I was doing exactly what he accused me of, producing the traumas that scarred him. But wait! I was also being Huck Finn, sticking out my tongue at him. Here I am miffed that Les didn't appreciate the great piece of therapy we just did. He thinks I did nothing, worse than nothing. Damn him! My odd remark also mirrors him, keeps things open, free. Far from knowing what's going on with him, I can't even figure myself out.]

Les: "You didn't help me last session. I tell you an important dream and you said nothing. All I got from you was bullshit. I went home and ruined our anniversary for my wife. I lectured her on how to bring the kids up, then tried to convince her our anniversary wasn't important. She writes letters about being starved for affection. She wants kisses, holding, normal things, which I don't want except for sex. I play analyst with her. With all these deep feelings I think I'm having, when it comes to a simple display of affection to my wife or any adult, I just don't.

"We were watching TV. She put her arm around me and I put mine around her, too, because I knew she wanted me to, but nothing else. She knew it. I've so much feeling, so much has come out in analysis. But these things that affect me, I don't show my emotions. I love Terry. I show feeling when I try to get someone into bed with me, but it's a show to try to get them to dig my act; afterwards it's a chore.

"I got affection from my mother. She didn't starve me. Same with father. My parents loved me and showed affection. But somewhere along the line something went wrong with my ability to show feeling. I can't give affection. I hear a voice inside me saying, 'I'm supposed to.' I'm supposed to show affection. Isn't that my mother demanding affection?"

M.E.: "Yes. It sounds like you're saying you hold back with Terry because your mother wants too much. I demand too much, too, (like your mother) and fail to show enough affection (like you with Terry). Shouldn't I have applauded you last time and told you what a good job you did? You needed to be admired, supported, cared for. I was wooden and lifeless. You were hurt and furious at the injury."

Les: "Aren't all these things supposed to come from childhood? Why do you bring yourself into it? I just want you to tell me why I do things, but I'm doing all the analyzing. Don't you do anything here? It can't all be tied to childhood. I tell my wife she was starved for affection in childhood and needs too much. I hug my boys spontaneously but not my wife. She wasn't starved in childhood and neither was I. I can't find anything in my past that accounts for my behavior. It's not that I'm a cold person. I'm a warm person but can't show it."

M.E.: "Like me."

Les: "Maybe it's not necessary to remember all the way back. Maybe it's just a matter of two or three years ago. Maybe it's now, not then. Maybe it all started when I was twelve, when the man next door died in a plane crash. If he hadn't crashed I wouldn't have to dredge up this stuff between my mother and I."

I was not doing a good job relating Les's fury to my injuring him. He danced about, using past against present and present against past. I was supposed to be a semi-omniscient interpretation machine feeding his mind knowledge about himself. I suspect when I did this it reinforced his ability to fly high above himself—knowledge over being. In his being he remained terribly conflicted about his mother, wife, me, work, everything. Knowledge was not enough. Something deeply experiential was needed, with and without knowing. I encouraged Les to speak more about his neighbor's crash, and he did. When he spoke himself out, I added, "Your mother's driving off and leaving you and your brother was like a crash?"

> Les: "You're doing it. You're doing it again, just like I said. What good does it do? You'll say that a good deal of what my mother did to me throughout my childhood was like a plane crash. That's analytic garbage."
>
> M.E.: "Was the pain analytic garbage, too?"
>
> Les: "The pain was real."
>
> M.E.: "The pain is real."
>
> Les: "Too real."

Les ended the session in tears. I could not avoid linking traumatic elements of childhood with the plane crash as symbol of horrific obliteration. Les quickly built on this, and rage turned to grief. He seemed to be saying, "Why disturb my relationship with my mother? Why stir up the pain I successfully dealt with by adapting to her demands and trying to become what I was supposed to?" At the same time he cried for his life, for his defensiveness, for his wounded self.

To get to himself, Les had to fight analysis. Analysis made demands. You were supposed to say what came to mind or whatever you liked. You were supposed to grow, to speak your truth, to become more yourself. There was such a gap between the analysis ideal and my faults and limitations. I starved Les by not feeding him enough meaning, support, or empathic regard and stuffed him with too many wrong things. If I commented on our relationship, I was in danger of taking analysis away from him, as his mother stole his life. If I commented on his history, I was in danger of depersonalizing our relationship and making him feel merely like a patient instead of a special person. There are so many ways to miss the boat.

Yet beneath variable successes or failures is a deeper therapy rhythm. One feels its pulsations beneath conceptual frameworks. Its ebb-flow, advance-retreat is deeper than any combination of particular meanings. Les reaches a high point, pulls back, seemingly undoes the good moment, then gathers himself up for another flying leap.

A wish comes true. He breaks through to limitless pain and weeps from the heart. He feels and shows emotion. Still this is not what he means by showing affection to his wife.

Love is the Center

During the next session Les spoke more of his terrors and need to love. The rise of feelings made him more afraid of dying.

Les: "I feel more. When I feel so much I'm afraid I'll go up in smoke. What if I die and leave my kids without a father? I love them so much. I don't want them to be hurt about anything. My wife says, 'You'll spoil the kids that way.' I say, 'Why should they know pain now? They'll have enough of it when they're older.' I can't bear the thought that they'll die someday. My terrors are abnormal, a nightmare. I try so hard to make sure they don't live a nightmare. I try to complete myself through my kids, to make myself whole through them. They're better versions of me."

M.E.: "The ideal you?"

Les: "The real me, the me I wanted so badly to be. The me with a Dad. With my Dad missing, something inside me was missing."

M.E.: "When your Dad disappeared, you disappeared?"

Les: "You know I've been angry! The closest I've come to real love is hooking up with my kids. Nothing, no one else does that for me. My mother didn't really show affection. Everything revolved around her. I give my kids what I wanted.

"Sometimes when I make love with Terry I just want to hold her. I had two uncles who always kissed me. I can't remember kissing my father. I miss my Dad. I'd like to hold and hug and kiss him and tell him, 'I love you.' He's getting old. We'll go through life shaking hands with each other. My brother and I shake hands. I kiss my mother on her cheek. I love these people. All the affection I never show goes on my kids. Then my wife accuses me of being unaffectionate. Not allowed to be anything but an image, you become an image. If I grabbed my mother and hugged her, she'd be embarrassed."

40

Defining Moments in Les's Therapy

M.E.: "What about your embarrassment?"

Les: "They'd be upset if I acted differently."

M.E.: "And your upsetment?"

Les: "You just can't take all these years and change them. My kids saved me from going dry. I can show myself with them. But that's not enough. There's part of my mother that is, I don't know, not sealed off—not inaccessible, but in some way not approachable. As if she lives in another kingdom, her own kingdom, and there is no room for me. Her ego demands loyalty from others and herself. Is there room for me in her throne room? I'm not going to get what I want from her. Deep inside her I feel love, but it does not reach the surface in the right way. I will never start living if I wait for her."

M.E.: "You speak of dying, your fear of dying. Yet I sense that the agony you speak of is more than death."

Les: "Maybe I was better off a couple of years ago when I didn't know I was miserable or why I was miserable. I picture myself with a cap and gown. There are two of me. The Les with a big REAL on my chest gives the other Les a diploma. Then the two become one. Clouds. A religious experience. Music playing, the song 'Come Fly With Me.' I'm nervous about flying again.

"Do you know I take you along when I fly? I used to take my mother. Now I hold on to you. She thinks you're a crutch. I told her I need a crutch. 'Les, you can get over it,' she says. She can't understand anyone who's not fearless and strong like herself. She thinks if I use her as a crutch, I won't need you."

Les spoke of various forms of aloneness. How alone he felt even so close to mother, how alone without a father. Les's father left the family when Les was in high school. He remarried and built a life in another part of the country. He could not compete with Bess for family dominance and resented taking a back seat. For years he waited for the time when he could leave.

For a time he tried his best not to be drowned out, but the fighting was too bitter. He gave up to keep peace but never entirely abandoned contact with his children. To the extent that he was able, he played with them, took them to ballgames, and showed interest in them. But his subordinate status definitely left a hole in the boys' lives. He left the family mentally long before his body did. I suspected Les might have made a go of his business after college if his father had been there to encourage him. This was not possible, and a wound took the place where a father might have been.

Nevertheless, Les did get things from his father. And he saw from his father's actions that it was possible not to give up, to go after what one wanted even if it took a long time. His father did make a life for himself, even if it was not in his first marriage. This hurt, but showed one did not have to die out. There *was* life outside or beyond mother. One *could* fly away, and that thought was frightening and hurtful, yet also freeing.

Much could be said about Les's relationship with his father. Les drew on strands of it in analysis and struggled to constitute a viable sense of father in his life. But the current focus is on his battle with mother and a long-delayed battle with himself.

The increased intensity of Les's feelings made alone-ness (mother-and-father aloneness and his own aloneness) more apparent. My remark that there were fears worse then death fell flat, but Les made better use of me in building himself up and drawing lines of battle. There was special urgency in Les's talk about love during this session. He wanted to convey its centrality for his existence and the challenges it set. He contrasted his mother's ego (per-haps ego in general) with living from the heart. Les tapped the well of love deep in his parents but did not want to be trapped by their personalities or his. He saw the differ-ence between his mother's need for him to be involved with her and simple expressiveness. He hoped to undo a lifetime of being like his parents, unable to express affec-tion. Anything less felt like a sour compromise.

Mind-Body Splits

Several weeks later Les took his family on a business trip to San Francisco. I thought it too long a trip for a first attempt to fly with his family, and his wife felt the same way. The children were excited, but Terry was furious that he would use them as guinea pigs. Les was head-strong, and insisted, "What good is analysis if I only get better in fantasy? It has to be real, or what good is it?" It turned out Les was right and we were wrong. But the trip also had a sobering effect on Les, since it led him to revisualize what he meant by cure.

In the session after the trip, Les developed a remark-able portrayal of his shakiness in terms of mind-body splits. I thought it the closest he had come to reading his psychic structure and experiencing the fault lines of his psyche. Like his encounter with the guide, boat, and snakes, it marked a point of no return, an increment in his ability to perceive and tolerate himself.

Les: "I did it on my own. It was my idea. Terry said, 'You have to prove yourself this way? You have to make us all go through it?' She was mad. What if I failed? What if I panicked and went crazy and drank myself to oblivion or pissed all over the floor? I get hysterical."

M.E.: "They've seen you that way many times."

Les: "Not the way I get when I fly. They hear about it. They haven't seen the worst. No one's seen the worst because most of it goes on inside me. Only bits of it get out. I look nervous. I sweat. I sound hysterical. But I pass. My behavior stays within bounds. Inside I'm a total wreck.

"I got the idea because of something you said a few weeks ago. You said I'm more afraid of something than death itself. It suddenly came to me it was no big deal, taking my kids on a flight. I got a gut feeling that said, 'You're not going to die.' But the other voice was there too. 'You're going to die.' If I *really* thought I was going to die, I wouldn't go. The trip went well."

M.E.: "So I'm not seeing a ghost."

Les: "No. I lived. I kept thinking all that was bothering me was a phobia used as a symbol for something else. I wasn't really going to die. I tried to think of what really was triggering me off. Thinking it must be something else would lessen my anxiety.

Defining Moments in Les's Therapy

"I slept the night before, but earlier I cried hysterically. What would happen if I lost control on the plane with my boys there? Then I thought what a straitjacket being strong was, my strong mother. What an impoverishment to just be strong. If I cry, okay. I saw myself crying and my embarrassment. Is that part of what I call dying?

"In a way I'm glad Terry was irritated. I didn't need her support and hugs in order not to crumble. I was full of excitement about the plane ride. For me feelings of excitement turn into doom. Something pleasant about to happen changes into a dread of something horrible. This time the fear of dying didn't do me in. I didn't lose myself in the dread that this is it. I wasn't always fully myself though. But what is myself?

"At first I watched the take-off from far away, higher than the plane. Down below I could see the plane and my body. This is something I do when I fly. When I'm above everything I keep the plane flying with my thoughts. My mind never stops. I believe if I stop thinking the plane is flying for a moment, it will crash. I must not let down."

M.E.: "It's up to you."

Les: "My mind whirls. That's when I start drinking heavily, to slow it down, blot it out. Below I see my body writhing, jerking, throwing a fit in the aisle. Completely hysterical."

M.E.: "Mind control and body chaos go together."

Les: "I never saw it that way, but yes. That's the picture. That fits, in a nutshell."

M.E.: "It's not clear to me whether the body splatter is contagious and floods the mind, or whether the mind spins off on its own, owing to the impossible effort it must make, or some combination."

Les: "Everything gets swept away by panic. But the me high above goes into a spin from working so hard to keep the plane up. My mind's a kind of plane above the plane that goes into a tailspin. I work harder and harder to stop the crash. I get out of it by drinking myself into a stupor. Why not take control by drinking? I'll end in oblivion anyway."

M.E.: "Really? It doesn't seem as if your oblivion comes after the crash, but blots out parts of a catastrophic process. The splitting you hope will save you turns into a spin. But the details of this business are obscure."

Les: "Thank God that on my trip with the boys the splitting didn't turn into spinning. It didn't go on so long. The plane rocked a little, and I said, 'Oh no. I'm going to lose control, get smashed, sick.' Then I said, 'Oh no. I'm not going to.' I felt relaxed and walked around, talked to the pilots. Terry enjoyed herself, too, but I swear she almost seemed angry at me for not needing her. But we all had a good time. It turned out the way I hoped it would, the way I wanted it to."

M.E.: "Isn't it amazing how worlds can switch in an instant? One moment you're about to crash, the next you're having a good time. I think that's great, but I'm not satisfied."

Les: "I got all this down on tape before it vanished, before the sick self attacked it. I felt good, but I expected an attack. Now you're attacking me. But I did have another fear in the back of my mind. While I was

enjoying myself, I got the thought it's so much better to
be like this than feel odd, unfamiliar, warped, or worse.
It was better to be sociable and walk around and talk to
everyone than feel I wasn't me somehow.

"I was afraid—I couldn't have said so then—that
the splitting and splattering would reach such a point
that I could no longer recognize myself. I would
become someone, something else. I would be totally
deformed or, I don't know—I picture science fiction
blobs or monsters or outer space creatures, aliens. I
would not be me."

M.E.: "Haven't you often said you were a shell that covered your mother?"

Les: "This was even worse. Like living double, seeing
double. That doesn't sound so bad when I say it. I can't
get to it."

M.E.: "You're trying to."

Les: "I asked Terry if she was surprised that I could do
it. Was she surprised that I got helped? She said no, she
wasn't surprised I could do it but wondered what analysis had to do with it. She's always wondering what good
is this doing me? What good can seeing all these feelings do? I get tools from analysis. I'll never be the world's
greatest flyer. I'll never find it easy to hop in a plane
and go from place to place. I'll always have to work at
it. But I'm a little stronger. I can do more.

"I'm not ready for a swing-down battle with my
mother yet, but it'll come when it's ready. It happened
with flying. The time was right for me. It's not so much
the flying but a definite growth process in me. I give a
lot of credit to analysis. I'm able to talk with myself, to

hear the good and bad voices and not simply get stuck in their battles. To grow you've got to sometimes go out and try things, like this plane trip. You have to find out where you are and push a little. You have to test your analysis in the real world.

"Before I come here, Terry asks, 'Are you going Tuesday? Nothing you do ever ends?' Analysis never ends. Terry and I are friendly enemies. I haven't told you for a while, but she throws things at me when she's mad enough. I'm almost afraid to say it, but after the trip she beat my back with a hammer, then burst out crying. Feeling the strong me threw everything off for her. I told her being stronger doesn't mean I won't need her, but maybe I won't need her in my sick way."

M.E.: "You mean, whether we're strong or not, we still need each other?"

Les: "We'll always need each other as persons."

Les's plane trip with his family was quite a triumph. Les needed to let others know the worst in him. He was determined to link inner with outer reality. He wanted to be able to express affection, but also terror. As things turned out he was lucky; he was also able to share joy.

An earlier remark of mine (ignored at the time) spurred Les's awareness that what he called dying referred to psychic, not merely physical, death. Les began to delineate the psychic death he dreaded. A sharp split took place between mental and physical aspects of himself. An observing mind flew high and watched his body below. At first this split provided Les with relief by giving distance from his situation. However, the split turned into a gruesome whirl. Les had to keep the plane up by mental effort. He did not trust body functions. He used his body as a performance machine and feared rebellion. To offset fear of failure, he accelerated mental activity. The race to oblivion was on.

Les usually diminished the agony of this process by creating his own oblivion, the stupor of liquor. He never allowed the split-spin to run its course. The horror of what might happen was intolerable, so the possibility of rebirth was foreclosed.

During the airplane trip with his family a miracle happened. He subdued the dread of catastrophe with social enjoyment. Good feelings washed away bad. This was a real achievement, although one cannot expect pleasant social feelings to be a solution to catastrophic dread. More work was needed for Les to develop taste and tolerance for the fall-apart/come-together rhythm of growth processes.

Terry was extremely open in her misgivings and fury. She was genuinely threatened and showed it. This was in sharp contrast with Les's mother, who pulled Les's emotional strings in ways he found hard to combat. With Terry, give and take was possible. Les and Terry really liked each other. He was able to say, perhaps for the first time, that he needed her for herself, not just because of illness. She was used to nursing him to health and was afraid of not being needed.

My affirmation of the value and reality of personal ties dovetailed with Les's basic vision, which he was daring to test out. The personal-communal dimension survives the ruthless struggle for individuation and makes individuation work.

Neville the Devil

A few months after the family plane trip, Les reported what turned out to be the culminating dream of his therapy.

> Les: "In the dream, Terry and I were in a big room at a psychedelic resort. A drug was piped through the ventilator system. There were hundreds of people in a stoned-type atmosphere.
>
> "A strange man with piercing eyes kept staring at Terry. He kept asking her to smoke with him. She finally decided to go with him to have a cigarette. I told her, 'Don't go.' She left. The room started to spin like a carousel, at first slowly. The doors were stationary; only the inside part of the room moved. I was looking for Terry but she wasn't there. The person she left with was called Neville. I was searching. The room was a complex, futuristic 'Clockwork Orange' place. I looked the whole day and couldn't find Terry or my kids.
>
> "I called the authorities, but they said there was nothing they could do. I kept searching. In the distance was a huge tower, like an erector set mountain, and on it was a strange platform and weird house—where Neville lived? I climbed the tower by grabbing onto metal pieces that jutted out. On the top were my children, somewhat beaten and emotionless. They looked at me with disbelief, as though they decided that this ghastly existence was their plight. I held them, and they cried and told me to take them away from there. They said Neville was on the other side of the platform. They warned me he was strong.
>
> "Terry was beaten a lot. Her dress was open, black. She was pregnant. She told me to take the boys and leave. She can't go. She's here with Neville. I took the boys

50

and began climbing down. Neville came after the boys, and the two of us fought. Neville knocked me off the tower. The boys climbed down. We got to the bottom at the same time.

"I told a friend about Terry's plight. He said he was a black belt and could help, so we climbed back up. Neville was ready and threw my friend off the mountain, then started beating me. I yanked Neville's arm and it came out of his body. It wasn't a real arm. He fell. He wasn't a man at all. I ripped out his limbs and beat him. Terry's expression and emotion started coming back, like normal. I ripped Neville apart in a crazy frenzy. I took Terry and started climbing down.

"I didn't think I could do it, but I did. I thought my friend—you—had the power. But I had it myself. I had to use it myself. Neville the Devil. Devil eyes and power. But it was all fake. I've been doped up all my life, but I'm coming out of it. Neville can only beat us as long as we're drugged. I've more power than I know how to use. I saved those dearest to me. The worst in me didn't win out."

For years, Les spoke of a fight he was not ready for. At last the battle was joined. He was used to losing in nightmares. Now he had climbed the tower and fought to the finish and won. He had come through his worst fears.

Who is Neville the Devil? The evil father (like the giant in "Jack and the Beanstalk"), his mother's power, the evil therapist, his own shadow? Everything destructive in life and himself? Perhaps Neville was related to the snakes of the earlier boat dream, the force of many snakes gathered into one powerful figure. Perhaps Les's whirling, spinning mind had gathered itself together in concentrated form.

51

More important than the *particular* power or force Neville the Devil represented was his function as *force or power as such*, in this case evil force or power. So much of Les's life was spent battling a force bent on destroying everything. It was as if something in Les were determined to pull him apart, grind him to pieces, render him less than nothing. And now this force assumed the form of a superpower, a monster, a devil, a specific attacker that could be attacked.

The dread of catastrophe that permeated Les's life was given a shape and name. Les's panicky rage and strength poured out against it. For a moment he let himself go completely. He could scarcely believe he won. It felt like a victory over everything he was afraid of.

Was the victory real or a hoax? Was Les kidding himself? Surely such a moment can't last. The destructive force will come again, perhaps worse than ever. One does not annihilate fear and catastrophe once and for all.

Yet something decisive happened. To have won even for a moment made all the difference in the world. Les could not pretend such a moment did not exist. Unless he betrayed himself, this moment would have to be part of further growth processes.

There was also a note of humor in the dream, albeit black humor. Neville the Devil is a name the dream made up, and it sounds a bit funny. The devil has the same name as a Catskill resort, and the dream, in fact, begins in a resort. The dreamer seems to confuse psychedelic drugs and dope, since the former may heighten consciousness rather than numb it. The important thing is that the dreamer represents Les as drugged out of existence, sleepwalking through life. Les has to wake up and face the worst, at least in his dreams. The dream indeed wakes Les up.

There is a cartoon quality to the dream. Les takes himself so seriously. He is gripped in cosmic struggle, the stuff of tragic myths. Yet one almost hears a Broadway orchestra in the background: Fighting the devil—Neville the Devil—New York style. The dream parodies or mimics Les's heroic battle, as well as valorizes it. Les the hero beat the supervillain; a note of hysteria runs through the anguish and victory. It is difficult to avoid sensing something juvenile in Les's heroic stance. The form of victory is one side against the other, this versus that, a sort of paranoid victory over paranoia. Did therapy reinforce his controlling attitude, his top-dog/underdog approach to relationships? Was he still mama's little boy, beating all odds, perhaps turning the tables on mama herself?

There was something grandiose and self-serving about Les's beating Neville by himself. No hero vanquishes the destructive force once and for all, not on this earth, and certainly not alone. Yet Les gained something from his breakthrough. He journeyed upwards-downwards through mind-body divisions and traversed anxieties related to up-down movement: heaven-hell, manic-depressive swings, inflation-deflation, thinking-feeling, give and take between the sexes, child-adult aspects of self, and so on.

Whatever the comic elements, Les moved from resort to tower, the seat of a devil's power, and returned to earth with a sense of renewal. Les and his family came through horrific dangers, a kind of death-rebirth experience. The Les who came down from the tower with his wife and children was not quite the same as the Les who lost them.

In the wake of this dream, Les began talking about dropping out and taking his family on a long camping trip. They would become vagabonds, live in a camper, travel through the country. His love of nature told him he did not have to be a grind. He did not have to twist himself out of shape in the corporate structure. After thoroughly indulging fantasies about being on the road and thawing out, he imagined what he really wanted was to own a small business in a small country town. He lived with this idea for two years before making it real.

Getting on Track: Personalizing Materialism

It took two years of therapeutic struggle after the Neville the Devil dream for Les to reach the point of feeling the time had come to act.

> Les: "I think of going to Vermont or Maine and opening a clothing or sports store. I won't tell Mom until our plans are underway. No big show; just do it. Fighting her every step of the way would put me in a little boy role. What will Terry say? Is it fair to uproot the boys?"

As might be expected, Terry was wary of Les's desire to make a new start but did not strongly oppose it. She adopted a wait-and-see attitude. Les did preparatory work, and soon Terry threw herself into it. The idea of moving away seemed to provide an opening for both of them. They chose a town in Vermont, and in less than a year bought a house and opened a store. Terry played a central role in making the store possible and successful. She helped run it and discovered she had natural ability in small business.

I was frightened by the radical change in Les's life. Would he try his wings and crash? He had a secure job he could use as a base for other jobs. Had analysis precipitated a mania that could destroy his financial capability? People's lives were at stake.

I also felt like cheering him on. Wasn't he finally doing what he wanted to, what he came to me for? Wasn't this *it*?

Les shared my realistic fears but did not look back. Fear slid into deeper terrors that threatened his momentum. For a time, Les drove back and forth between New York and Vermont and fought private battles. A voice told him leaving would kill his mother or himself. Another voice told him nothing of the sort would happen. "I was terrified she would get a heart attack or stroke or throw her arms around my legs and plead with me and make an awful scene or turn into a witch and mutilate me. Each time I drove to Vermont and back I half expected to have a terrible accident. The car would veer off the side of the road or crash into a truck. It would have a mind of its own. I wouldn't be able to control it. I was surprised each time I made the trip without cracking up and actually enjoyed the drive. I couldn't believe she didn't care, that life, her life, went on as usual. Am I more shocked to find I can do without her, or she without me?"

Which was worse, killing each other or being able to live without each other? Les finally admitted that life away from home made his mother most happy. For so long their special fusion or imaginary closeness had both paralyzed and empowered him. He thought it was everything to her, that she treasured it beyond all things. "Yet I always knew this was the way it would be. I heard a whisper saying, 'She'll get along. She's got her life; that's what really matters.' I guess I didn't really want to believe it. I wanted to think I mattered more to her than she did to herself."

For a while Les saw me whenever he came to New York on business. His visits became more infrequent, and for a couple of years I received only several calls. I was surprised to hear from him five years and then again eight years later, for brief consultations. His business was successful. He and Terry loved the work, and their marriage was thriving. In one of his consultations, he sought to bolster his courage to open branches in other towns. Another visit was mainly concerned with his children.

Old fears of flying or for his children did not vanish, nor did quarrels with his wife. But they became more manageable and better absorbed in the larger personal space that Les had carved out. Les's lifespace as a whole became one he could identify with, one he could say yes to, one he played a central role in creating.

A basic irony was that this man who so needed to control was so close to being out of control. Les remained addicted to the need to control, although in a roomier way. I would have liked him to do more work with elusive fears, such as intimations of being a blob or misshapen, or being someone or something else, a monster, an alien. There was much Les did not face. Analysis did not remake him. A basic gain in analysis was for Les to take control in a way that cooperated with the main axis of his life, so that he and his life fit each other better and stood a better chance of working in tandem. Les felt more open, in spite of his need for control. In one of his last visits, he said, "What amazes me is the strength I draw from everything that wounded me. I can't really know what happened, can I? I'm less afraid of not fitting together. All the parts do not exactly come together. I'm less afraid of scatter, and that somehow helps me find my way."

One wonders what analysis does, how analysis works. I can agree with Les, "I can't really know what happened, can I?" Yet changes happen and one gets ideas about them. Above all, analysis provided a place and atmosphere for Les to contact himself and grow into this contact. All through his life he sensed something wrong and diagnosed himself, yet could do little about it. As the years went on, his wheels kept spinning in the same circles. Talking with friends and family did not change things.

One can speak truth in analysis with less fear than at the home or office. One can try, as much as one is able, to speak the whole truth, better than in a court of law, because one can take time. All one's inconsistencies and contradictions will be valued rather than torn to pieces, because *we are inconsistent and contradictory*. In analysis, we do not have to pretend otherwise.

We can begin to let down, thaw out, take time out from official versions of ourselves. So many voices come up: the voices of one's parents, mate, children, bosses, so many alternative voices of one's own. Main lines of self gradually gather strength and say, "Hey ! Over here! Try us! We're your real you!" It's hard to believe one survives the abuse one's been put through, and one's own abuse of self. The miracle is that one keeps breaking through one's own unreality.

What is different about analysis? The analyst knows about family politics, ego, wounds, bisexuality, rage, desire, longing, need, pride, psychic structures, unconscious processes, transformational-transitional spaces, on and on. The analyst knows he is exempt from nothing and may be part of the disease. We are all in the business of growing equipment to support ourselves and others, to support mutual evolution. And we are all learning how this is done.

How odd that a profession specializes in this task that is common to all of us. Analysis itself is not immune from inconsistency and contradiction. They are its lifeblood and pulse. Perhaps the analyst, unlike mate or parent, does not expect consistency. Analysis provides a situation outside daily battles so that the story of these battles can be told and, in part, reenacted. Something grows that is more than the sum of one's battles, a kind of resetting of personality, a shift of attitude and direction. The analyst knows there is always another position, something unstated, deviant, something that does not fit in. The analyst expects paradoxes that no one can live with.

Perhaps most important of all, psychoanalysis provides a background for moving back and forth between positions. In time, one's unconscious begins to process life better. One learns to rely on one's unconscious to do more and better work, so that one does not have to do everything oneself. When this happens, one feels a deep support for leaps that make life worthwhile. One feels held in the depths of one's being, so that suspension of ego control is joyous.

Before analysis, Les never had a chance to stretch his psychic limbs and exercise imaginal life productively. In analysis, he could reach for the place nightmares come from and speak from the edge of his psychic universe. Les did not overcome his hero mania or grandiose self. His emotional life was melodramatic and sentimental. But enough of a shift occurred in his attitudinal framework for such raw materials to become more usable and less persecutory. He was better able to live from the heart, to personalize his world.

Les's soul bore the stamp "Made in the U.S.A." He was brought up to be successful. In one way or another his pleasures were materialistic, including a sort of emotional materialism. Yet a still, small voice nagged him. His way of life did not feel right. He hated his life of fear, his whorishness, his twisting himself out of shape to please his mother and bosses. Each failure to go to bat for his own ideas triggered waves of self-hate.

Analysis allied itself with his restlessness, his unease, the inner voice and promptings that egged him on. Our speaking inspired and maddened each of us and shifted the tone and direction of his materialism. Analysis enabled Les to work toward a better blend of love and ambition.

Les did not leave materialism behind. He loved making deals and maintaining a high standard of living. But he gained the satisfaction of being able to recognize himself in his work. He built a life that allowed him to exercise his abilities without injuring the next guy. His success was not achieved at someone else's expense. He felt better about himself. He enjoyed nature, family, business, and community. Love of life and work fit better because he was able to link materialism with personal values. Les carved out a place in which personal being had more of a say, in which personal identity mattered. That made all the difference.

Chapter Three

Key Stages in Lynn's Therapy

It was not immediately clear to me why Lynn sought help. She voiced discontent with her husband, work, brother, and mother. But she claimed to be happy enough and felt her life was basically positive. She did not give me any particular reason for wanting psychotherapy, but my inclination was to see her anyway.

Her face was bony and her voice sharp; her body seemed tense and alive. She had a strong New York accent, which fascinated me but which I did not care for. It seemed to say, "Take me as I am, on my own terms, or lump it." I felt a little put off by its shotgun defiance. She seemed angry at me, as if I were forcing her to be here. Her voice intimated I was doing something wrong. Dare I question it? Would she know what I meant? Was I making it up? Did Lynn need to be threatening in order to feel comfortable?

She talked a lot about her brother Lou. He was finishing high school but often got into trouble. Lou was a liar and crook. His mother bailed him out of one jam after another, and Lynn wondered whether that was good. Perhaps it would be better if he got caught and suffered the consequences. Then he might get scared enough to face reality. Lynn worried and felt like beating his brains out to make him think right. She wanted to help him but did not know how.

> M.E.: "It sounds like Lou wants excitement and needs things in an uproar."
>
> Lynn: "I'm afraid he'll destroy himself."
>
> M.E.: "Does Lou carry the turbulence for the whole family, or does any of it burst out elsewhere?"

Lynn then spoke about her anger at her father, mother, and husband. She was angry at her father for not taking care of himself. He was a quiet man who tried to soothe everyone. He was too good. He got fatter and his heart got worse. Lynn was angry at her mother for being hysterical and ineffectual. She was angry at her husband Andy for being cut off from his feelings and spending most of his time trying to complete his doctoral work in American studies.

She also loved them all and wanted the best for them. She was a loyal, caring, and competent person. She enjoyed entertaining Andy's friends and colleagues. She was proud of him and her competence. She felt at ease meeting faculty members and liked the academic atmosphere. In addition to art and photography, Lynn taught high school history, and it made sense to her that she would end up with someone in a similar field on a more advanced level.

Key Stages in Lynn's Therapy

Lynn wondered if she should do more with her studies, although neither the grueling work nor the politics of the academic rat race appealed to her. She preferred to raise a family and enjoy intellectual stimulation through her husband's associations and pursue her interests more informally. She more or less felt that she had found her niche.

Lynn was apologetic about coming to therapy. She felt there was nothing bad enough in her life to justify the expense and effort. There was nothing she could not handle. But she could not dispel a nagging sense of wanting something more or better, as long as work, marriage, and family remained intact. She was proud of herself for trying to do more with her life, even if she did not want her attachments threatened. She saw therapy as an enlightened undertaking, a sophisticated thing to do. Her husband, on the other hand, found the idea of therapy abhorrent. Therapy was for sick people. He did not like a stranger meddling with his wife, marriage, and certainly not with his own most intimate being. Why fix what isn't broken?

Fire in the Basement

A frequent theme in Lynn's dreams involved danger to her husband. In one dream she and Andy put out a fire in the basement of their building, yet the fire somehow spread to the floor below her apartment. They could not put this fire out and had to leave the blazing building. Andy worried about his books and papers and tried to reenter the building. He was overcome by smoke and passed out, but firemen and other people helped and the fire was put out. Firemen administered oxygen to Lynn and Andy. A woman was in shock. Andy's glasses were ruined in the rubble. A fireman assured him that he would be able to get into the building and get his things out safely.

In the dream, Andy was more threatened by the fire than Lynn. He had more to lose—his doctoral work. The fire was Lynn's rage at Andy because of his absorption in his work, but it also involved more. Lynn felt more warmly about her family than Andy did to his. Andy resented her ties to her parents, brother, and sister. He wanted more attention and warmth.

Lynn felt Andy was too clinging, even cloying. He always wanted sex to be a big production. Lynn wished they could do it with less fanfare and mushiness. In intimate matters she was more matter of fact than Andy, and this pained him. He wanted to feel that everything was all right, and she resented having to pretend that things were better than they were. It fell on her to be the one to make bad feelings go away, and good feelings stay.

Andy was always going in and out of his work and in and out of his demand that Lynn be there for him. His wish to study suited Lynn fine. She had tasks and interests and liked time to herself. She hated the pressure of regulating time according to his needs. The rapid, intermittent nature of his rhythm bothered her.

Their sexual life led to bitter frustration. Lynn was orgiastic only on top, so that if she was to be fully satisfied she *had* to end every sex act on top. This bothered

Andy. Neither Lynn nor Andy seemed to mind taking turns on top, but they were unhappy with a state of affairs that forced them to choose who would be satisfied at a given time. It took away spontaneity and made them shy of sexual life, which was increasingly like combat.

In the dream Lynn and Andy, with help from others, put out the fire in the basement only to find that it had spread to another part of the building. Fire is passion, the uncontrollable. How fortunate that Lynn and Andy could not extinguish it, that it had a life of its own. Lynn was caught between its destructiveness and loss. The possibility of modulated heat taxed her resources.

Lynn felt cold when faced with Andy's angry, cloying demandingness. She was angry that he did not let her be herself. His stickiness did not leave room for her warmth to emerge. On the other hand, Andy felt she threw water on his enthusiasm. Because she felt pressured to be there for Andy, Lynn often turned off her emotions. She feared that her feelings were dying out. She did not like being a cold, angry, ungiving woman and was furious and pained at being forced into this role. Lynn did not want the fire in her basement to go out, but she did not want to be reduced to being a raging maniac.

She did not know what to do with her fire. In real life Lynn handled herself like a good fireman. She was realistic and prided herself on her ability to function. Nevertheless, she was bothered by sexual problems, rage, Andy's demands, her coolness, and difficulties in finding her own space. Everything worked well; nothing worked well enough.

Fire symbolizes disturbance, and Lynn partly connected with her difficulty by saying, "I see the building as the bond between Andy and me. It's the place where we live, and when it works well it's how we should be, the way Andy thinks it should be. I get objective and see burning spots." Andy's dream of paradise is spoiled by Lynn's ability to see that the building is burning. *Lynn's ability to see the fire is a disturbance, as is the fire itself.* Andy preferred to play disturbances down and make believe they did not exist.

The dream ends well enough. Lynn and Andy are safe. They come out on top. But there is also damage, danger, and ill health. An area of her personality is in shock and must be cared for. Andy's, or Lynn's, ability to see is further threatened by the loss of his glasses. His work is unharmed, and soon things will go on as usual. They survived the potentially catastrophic moment. But in psychic reality there are better ways to deal with fires than merely extinguishing them. As in external reality, fire contributes to many kinds of work.

I'll Be Worse Than Ever

Soon after the fire Lynn dreamt that she saw my name among other names, perhaps third or fourth on a list of prestigious people. She feared that I was becoming too important and worried that I would fail her. She linked me with firemen and other helpers in her dream and was glad for the help. But she feared what would happen if she became too dependent on me.

Key Stages in Lynn's Therapy

Lynn: "I don't want to find out you can't help me. In my dream, you (the firemen) help. But in real life my anger may be too much. Sometimes when I can't talk here I think you're just like Andy. You're secretly on his side; you're both men. Why should you be on my side? My anger grows with my silence. I want you to know this without my saying anything. I want you to talk and help me. I get angrier having to ask. That's what I feel with Andy. Now I feel there's so much at stake with my feelings.

"It's therapy magic. When I'm not here I feel therapy is nonsense, but once I come and get into it, nothing seems more important. Now I feel everything's at stake. One false move and the world of my feelings will fall apart or go wrong. Everything depends on getting it right.

"You make me angry when you don't say anything and I go on like this. You must know what you're doing. If I get angry at you there would be too much to lose. You want me to get angry at you. You think I'll lose out if I don't. You think I'm afraid I'll destroy therapy if I get angry. But that's intellectual. My fear that I'll lose out is real. I'm afraid to get near it. I get sad, tired. I fade away. My feelings die out. Blotto. Now I'm confused, now dead."

M.E.: "The confusion is alive or dead?"

Lynn: "It's going back and forth, not knowing what to think or feel. I don't know. There's too much anxiety and I kill it, or it's just too much and I drop out."

M.E.: "Do you turn off to get away from the confusion, or does the confusion spin you out of existence?"

Lynn: "What difference does that make? You're too mental, like Andy. Why do you want to know? The important thing is I get scared and go away. I vanish because my fury scares me."

M.E.: "You can't touch the fear? It's like getting electrocuted?"

Lynn: "Yes. I can't get near it. It's like a shock that never ends. I'm grateful to blot out. But blotting out makes me mad and scared too. I don't want to be dead."

M.E.: "You want me to help keep you in life but are afraid I'll cause you even more pain."

Lynn: "I'm afraid that if things get botched up here, the effect will be more devastating and I may never get on track. At least Andy can't deal with feelings, and I hate him for it, but I'm safe. Here there is the hope or pretense of being able to work with these things, and if it goes wrong, then what? I could end up worse than ever."

We neared the half-year mark and were getting started. Lynn described an interweaving of rage, fear, sadness, confusion, paralysis, numbness, dependency, loss, and hope. I was struck by her mixture of defensiveness and sensitivity. She shut feelings off, blamed others, organized herself around external problems, yet had a special talent for noting states of being. She became exquisitely sensitive to momentary shifts along the comfort-discomfort sensation spectrum and to rudimentary elaborations of psychical disturbances. I think it important to emphasize that she had never done this before; she had not focused on moment-to-moment fluctuations of sensations and emotions in a sustained way. It was a talent released by therapy, a hunger for self.

She began therapy by talking about the most obviously disturbing element in her family, her brother Lou. However, she soon let out a catalogue of disturbances related to husband, job, parents, life in general. The idea that disturbance was essential to self did not occur to her. Disturbance was something to get rid of, to correct, to solve.

Lynn was able to link her sense of disturbance to therapy. She sensed how self rises and falls in therapy. She could give all, and I might fail her. Perhaps Lynn hoped therapy would save her. Such an overvaluation of therapy may be symptomatic of a weakened self but also bears witness to human longing. What an unpredictable mixture of failure and success living is! Therapy gave Lynn a chance to taste this mixture more thoroughly, to experience its nuances. It gave her time to be with herself in new ways, and she made use of it.

Different Kinds of Silence

Lynn continued talking about her anger, confusion, and silences. She tied some of her states to my behavior and personality but also found herself drawn to aspects of her past that lived in the present. Following is an excerpt from a session several weeks after the one just described. My notes begin after I got up to get a tissue. Usually I kept one box near me and one by Lynn, but I had left mine on the table.

Lynn: "You had to get up, and I forgot what I was going to say. We were talking about anger. Something about my anger when I was a kid, which I feel towards you. My mother was telling me a story. Now I can't remember, and it makes me furious that you can do that to me, that you can make me do that to myself."

M.E.: "We have control over it?"

Lynn: "Now I think of my sister [Adrienne] and Josh [Adrienne's son]. She works a few days a week, and my mother stays with Josh. I like my sister. She's impulsive, shows her temper. What she feels at the moment is what comes out. It's jumpy, crazy. She and Josh fight and make up fine. It annoys my mother. My mother says she shouldn't show such anger to Josh; he's only a baby. Josh takes both his hands and hits my mother in the face for not allowing him to have something. My sister gets angry. My mother tells Josh, 'No. You shouldn't do that. I love you.' My sister lets him feel as he will. They get angry, they make up. My mother thinks this is terrible and starts to make him act nice. She took his hand to make nice to her face saying, 'Grandma loves you.' He hugged and kissed her! But he usually does that when he feels it.

"I started thinking of my angry feelings, her ways of dealing with them: 'Behave; be nice.' It annoyed me. I like my sister's way better. I like her way and not my mother's at all. If that's the way she handled anger when we were kids—be nice! Now I go blank and lie here not thinking of anything. I can't tell if my anger made me blank or if I had nowhere else to go.

70

[After long, silent moments.] "I am still absolutely blank. The only thing I'm thinking about is how come I don't feel stuck thinking about nothing. I don't feel stuck and don't feel confused. I kept thinking if I felt stuck I'd ask for help to get unstuck. But I don't feel stuck, yet fear I'm wasting time."

M.E.: "What makes you feel not talking is a waste of time?"

Lynn: "That's the reason I didn't say anything right away. I wasn't sure I wasn't wasting time. But the longer I stayed that way I felt I'd be wasting time if I stayed too much with it.
[More silence.] "I feel a little light-headed. I'm not on solid ground, as though if I stand up I'll feel okay again. I can't think of anything except how I feel about not thinking anything, and I can't feel how I feel about it except that what I didn't mind at first seems to be bothering me more." [More silence.]

M.E.: "I'm wondering which silence you're falling into now. Did I get you off the track? You began angry at me, then your mother, then came a peaceful, quiet time and now a disturbance again."

Lynn: "I'm wondering why you decided to speak out and interrupt me at this time?"

M.E. "Did I interrupt something—the disturbance? I ended the tension?"

Lynn: [Laughs.]

M.E.: "What were you into? I botched it up? Were you annoyed?"

71

Lynn: "I wasn't into anything. I was just expecting you not to say anything unless I did first. You surprised me. Actually I was starting to feel worse—light, a floating head only. I was going to ask you to talk. I was stuck. I was glad, relieved you came in. It made me feel better. What is this? A moose?" [Lynn picked up a stuffed animal I had in the room for play therapy with children.] "It has antlers. I was looking at it when I started floating. I was looking for something to hold on to—your books, table. Then my eyes spotted this one. Then you spoke and I relaxed more. Now I feel happy, together, fresh."

Lynn moved from fury at me and her mother into a peaceful silence, followed by a more formless disturbance that I broke up. It seemed that I had provoked her anger by getting up and getting a tissue. I do not know which she was madder at: her failure to control me or my insensitivity. Since she had access to her fury, I decided to respond to the hidden ideal of mastery that tinged her talk. She felt she ought to be master of her memory and not subject to the effects of my capricious movements.

After I wondered aloud about the importance of mastery, Lynn's fury shifted from me to a recent memory of her mother's inadequate response to baby anger. Although my remark deflected her fury from me, a more detailed picture of maternal fear, control, and brain-washing (making baby nice, corruption through love) appeared. Then Lynn went blank, and we did not know whether her blankness warded off further evolution of the scene with her mother or had another function. If I had asked her to stay with her feelings for her mother in face of the blankness, she doubtless would have made the effort. But the blankness seemed to be positive in itself. It was a peaceful, refreshing blankness, although it degenerated into uneasy floating.

It appears I was guilty of provoking or colluding with two deflections: her fury at me became fury at mother; her fury at mother was followed by blankness. However, the benefits were significant. Lynn experienced a fuller sense of what she went through growing up and for some moments was able to relax deeply. Her blankness was alive and resonant before she began to break apart again. For the moment her need to be in control dropped away.

On her way out, Lynn remarked that she felt less "thin." She had always felt that she "looked thin" next to her sister. She saw Adrienne as fuller, more real, and herself as the withdrawn one. Lynn wanted to be more like Josh and Adrienne, and as she got up to go was surprised that she was feeling the aliveness she envied.

More Silence, Fury, Chatter, and Fear of Madness

The next session occurred a week later and began with a gabby account of worries. Once Lynn got the worries off her chest, she made her way to an impasse point.

> Lynn: "I'm disappointed with my grade in lab. I only got a B and bombed out on the final so will get a C in the course. I don't know whether I deserved a C, but I know I'm going to get one. [Lynn was taking some graduate courses in order to better her position.] I don't know why I can't stop yawning. I've been feeling pretty

down this week. I felt let down after the tests. That happens after pressure builds up. I'm yawning again [laughs]. I'm relieved they're over.

"I just came from my allergist and on the ride over wondered if my allergies get worse when I try to think of something to talk about here. I rarely do that now. I just come without thinking about anything. I used to get tense thinking about what I was going to say. Now there's another kind of tension. I can't think of anything.

"In my car the same thing happened as in last session. I was thinking about nothing. Nothing. And in the waiting room I wanted to run away. I don't know. That's all I've got to say. Nothing else. That's it, the place where I'm stuck. I don't know what to do with it, but that's *IT*. I wanted to run away at the thought of going back to the place where I'm stuck. I'm stuck, and I'm going to be stuck, and that's not a word I'm used to using. That's not a word I've used in a long time. [That is, Lynn was used to being on top of things.] I'm nervous about the whole thing. I don't know what to do about it anymore.

"I wonder if it's my mother wiping my mind out. A lot of doors are slamming around here today. My sister just lets Josh know she's angry or lets him know she's hurt. 'You hurt mommy, Josh, so I'm putting you down.' My mother would make believe nothing was happening to her and con his feelings.

"She's making a mess of a possible vacation for me. I have a chance to take a couple of weeks off and go to Europe. Now my mother's talking about an uncle who can get me a cheap flight. But everything's wishy-washy, and I've got to talk to the assistant principal if I'm going to go. I was talking to Andy about it, and he was nudging me to cement this. I screamed at him, 'If you say one more word about it, I'm going to kill you.' It was one of the few times he didn't keep on. It stuck in my mind as being different.

Key Stages in Lynn's Therapy

M.E.: "Your scream worked."

Lynn: "This time. Usually it doesn't. Usually we go on and on. Something was different. *My fury came out of the same place I get stuck in here.* It wasn't simply me against him or him against me. *My fury came out of nothingness,* yet my mother triggered it off. I wasn't in a knock-down battle with Andy. I paused, waiting to get it back, but he shut up. A terrific sense of power. It's the first time I felt that. I don't think I ever shut him up before. Maybe he thought I was going to kill him somehow.

"I taught today for the first time this week. I took a few days off because of the exams and felt paranoid about calling in sick and guilty about a friend taking my classes. She was a doll, but some of the other teachers said, 'Watch out, she'll tell the principal.' I'll trust her. She promised to take my classes if I go to Europe. We hit it off. She's an administrator who makes it worth dealing with the shit you have to take, all the screaming. She's really good. [Silence.]

"What I feel is I want to keep talking, but I can't think of anything to talk about. [Silence.] I feel like something is on the verge. [Silence.] I need help—anything but being stuck. I'm getting exhausted."

M.E.: [Is Lynn retreating from her sense of power? After talking about her power she spoke about trust. Was it too much to keep up? Her silence became difficult rather than pleasant. She is back to where she is stuck. Should I ask about her feelings toward me? I feel I want to ask about her body. Where is her body in all this?] "Can you say where you're most exhausted?"

Lynn: "All over but mostly my shoulders and chest."

75

M.E.: "Can you get more in your chest?"

Lynn: "All I want is to run away from the feeling of being stuck—anything but feeling stuck. When I feel my breathing I feel like a balloon, a balloon that won't burst but just shakes. I wonder if I should think something, but there's nothing in my mind. Just pure feeling, like something building up. I'm not sure. A really down feeling. [Cries.] I didn't think I'd start crying. I don't know why."

M.E.: "What's wrong with crying?"

Lynn: "Nothing. But I couldn't. That's what's wrong. I couldn't cry unless someone pushed a pin. I didn't expect it to just come. I don't know exactly what I want, or what to ask for, or what I need to look for, or anything. I don't know me anymore. I'm not the me I thought I knew. I'm not used to crying for no reason. I talked to keep myself in the room. When I was quiet I just wanted to stay in the room. It didn't matter what I said or didn't say as long as I didn't go out of the room."

M.E.: "Where are you now? Are you still here?"

Lynn: "No. I don't know. I feel it draining out, all out the wrong end. It just dissolved. I feel real cold."

M.E.: "I wasn't right for you somehow. Maybe I'm cold."

Lynn: "I hear words that I'm thinking, and they sound very silly: 'I lost life lenses.' Life. I don't know. I was feeling too much. It was too exhausting. Then I started to feel relaxed, more comfortable, because it was draining out. Now it doesn't feel so good. Whatever it is feels silly. Happy. Silly is the wrong word. I'm afraid I'm going to leave without ever knowing what it was about."

M.E.: "Lenses have to do with seeing. Maybe something about not being able to feel and see at the same time."

Lynn: "I wrote something about Josh and my mother and didn't want to show it to you. I felt vulnerable. I want to show it to you."

M.E.: "You want me to see it. You want us to be able to see *and* feel."

Lynn: "I showed you one thing I wrote, something weird, and you liked it. I thought you'd be pissed."

M.E.: "You can get addicted to the relief of the bad thing not happening."

Lynn: "I really thought you'd like it, but I didn't want you to see it. I don't know. I feel that if I relax for a minute I'm going to go bananas."

M.E.: "Maybe you think I see too much and will take your craziness away from you."

Lynn: "I'm not holding myself so tightly. I'm going to go bananas. I could hold myself tighter and stop this. I'm in the middle now, not too tight or loose. I feel I'm one of those toys that balances on top of a glass and goes up and down and never falls, never stays still. A bird dipping its beak, back and forth. [Laughs wildly, then cries and laughs wildly.] I feel I'm going crazy. I never did this before."

The session ended with Lynn's sensation of going crazy. Her blankness became hysterical, not simply angry, peaceful, or uncomfortable. Uncontrollable laughing and weeping erupted. Perhaps this was what she meant earlier when she said that something was building and on the verge.

Lynn's dip into emotionality involved anger and sexuality. Early in the session she wondered if her mother killed off her mind. She spoke of rage at her mother and fury with Andy. In past sessions she expressed anger at me for making things hard for her. As noted earlier, her sex life was beset with difficulties. I do not want to minimize the relationship between madness and problems with rage and sexuality. Lynn feared rage and sexuality and their consequences. Nevertheless, Lynn's inchoate emotionality and fear of madness involved more than blocked rage and sexuality.

The more general difficulty of emotional communication arose. Lynn fell into a realm of experience for which she lacked communicative tools. She talked too much and then became tongue-tied upon discovering her raw emotional life. She became aware of the gap between her ability to use words and her experiential flow. It was precisely because she saw that she could feel that she momentarily lost her ability to speak.

For much of her life, Lynn used words to stay on top of things. Words came easily to her. It would be too simplistic to say that her flow of speech was cut off from her feelings. What she said expressed her feelings, but in a way that kept her in a position of competency. When she spoke, her aim was to right herself, to get herself to feel good or appear in a good light. Words were used less as tools for exploration than to get rid of tension, a sort of social psychological gossip.

In itself this may be normal. It certainly is common. But Lynn brought herself into therapy and risked finding out how hard it can be to let go of superficial controls. Or, rather, she began to see how tenacious and deeply rooted "superficial" control of words and feelings can be.

She now came into contact with the quasi-fragmentary nature of experience and the awkwardness of fragmentary communication that is faithful to the moment. She calmed down somewhat before leaving my office and waited for a time in the waiting room. But she was afraid that if she completely righted herself something important would be lost. She was dipping her beak in and out of the water, still too rigidly perhaps. But the movement was meaningful to her.

Bucking the System: Creativity and Provocativeness

The following week, Lynn spoke about a conflict she had with the principal and department chairman at work. She supported a project that met with disapproval from her department chairman. The project meant a lot to Lynn, more than she realized at first. She began her session by speaking in a diffuse manner about her anxiety and rage at the stupid men at work.

Lynn: "I can't stop talking. I've been going on since Monday. Haven't felt well these past three days. I've been infuriated, uptight. A powerful situation. The chairman of my department feels powerless over a project I'm sponsoring. I let a student of mine, Mary, do an independent project instead of the history class. She's doing a photographic essay of parts of the city and making it into a kid's book with poems she wrote for the photos. She's really good. She has an intuitive feel.

"I got permission from the principal to do it. The department chairman found out and is furious. He didn't like the idea. I felt him out in the past, and he never liked the idea of substituting an independent project for a class. He's furious that I went over his head. He's pissed not only at me, but at the principal for doing something like this behind his back. I can't say I blame him, but he's an uptight asshole. He says Mary's not learning anything. The principal was caught between us and had to take his side. I can understand that, but the way he handled it was wrong. He kept saying, 'Never again.' I said, 'Yes, I will.' Then he yells, 'Who the hell do you think you are? I'm the boss here.'

"He could have been more diplomatic. He flew off the handle in front of others. He berated me every day this week, called me incapable, crazy. He tried to get the art teacher and another history teacher to agree, but they thought Mary's work was brilliant. Her work comes right from inside of her. Her work is sensitive, and she's vulnerable when criticized. The chairman attacked Mary when he saw her. He blamed her. She can't speak up to him like I can. I felt horrible. I had to convince her to get into it and stay with it. It was awful. He complains I use a specialty others can't teach efficiently. It's true Mary is doing what I like to do. I'm a pretty good photographer. I love it. I want to use all I have and am glad I can be there when someone like Mary comes along.

"I told the chairman that his idea of teaching was inefficient. He's angry he couldn't get me worried because I'm tenured. There's a running hatred between us now. But I'm not powerless. Now it's the other way around. There's nothing he can do. The question is how to stay out of his way; otherwise it'll be scene after scene.

"What's next? I had a snippet of a dream. A girl was going upstairs. I was helpful to her. She was nice. A man gets an erection.

"There's a lot of little pieces in my mind. I remember you saying you're not sure where to go. You said we'd have to discuss it, whatever it was. I felt insecure about your expressing uncertainty. It felt good, too. It was more honest and genuine than someone who already knows everything. Sometimes you sound so goddam right. It feels funny to feel two opposite things at the same time: security and insecurity. I guess I'm saying I want you to say something about my dream, but not too much."

M.E.: "You first."

Lynn: "The girl must be Mary, and I'm helping her. Then the stupid penis poses a threat, the stupid chairman and principal. They keep poking and sticking themselves into us. They get in the way and make me want to get away."

M.E.: "That's what happened in reality. But were there bad feelings in the dream?"

Lynn: "The dream felt nice."

M.E.: "Even the erection?"

Lynn: "The erection, too. I felt good when I woke up. It was a sexy dream but it wasn't sexy. It was a nice feeling, not mainly excitement. More like when something nice happens between people, something that fills you out."

M.E.: "Going upstairs and finding an erection was an expansion."

Lynn: "Yes. In the dream."

M.E.: "Stick with the dream."

Lynn: "I want to say bad things about the penis but have to force myself not to."

M.E.: "You want to fight the bad penises rather than enjoy your good one."

Lynn: "I want those bastards to get it, but there's no fighting in the dream."

M.E.: "You feel good about going to bat for Mary, sticking up for yourself and her. You feel pleased with your own good penis, your phallic power."

Lynn: [After a quiet pause.] "It's the first time in days I took a deep breath. I couldn't seem to relax lately. [Silence.] I'm in a funny spot. I'm not ready to let go of old things and start something new. [Silence.] I just stopped talking for the first time in a long time and felt I was relaxing for a minute. I wanted to tell you the dream but felt funny about it, like moving into something different, something I wasn't sure I wanted. Maybe I'm getting hooked into things that are happy, and I'm afraid I won't be able to let go of it."

Key Stages in Lynn's Therapy

M.E.: "You won't be able to let go of happiness?"

Lynn: "Maybe a new way of being happy. I fought for creativity in a way I never did before. I wasn't going to let him [the chairman] stiff Mary's creativity. His trying to stifle creativity is what really got to me. I almost forced her to do the project. Mary held back; she was afraid to do it, then poured her heart and soul into it. She works through her feelings *and* her head. She enjoyed the people she met around the city. It was a big thing for her, but she would have given in to the chairman. She didn't want trouble. I pushed her to see it through, and once her own drive took over she was terrific. I was able to buck the system because of Mary. I used her, I guess. She was me, and I she. I needed to feel that kind of freedom. But she got a real boost, too. I lived through her, but now she knows what she can do. Just try and stop her from doing more."

There was more than a touch of bravado in Lynn's declaration, but something substantial as well. There would be time to ferret out whatever need she had to provoke and taunt authorities, or explore her rage at males. Surely she felt hemmed in by male authorities, whom she regarded as pigheaded and arbitrary. But what needed support now, above all, was her drive to side with creativity, even if through a proxy. She encouraged Mary to do what she herself failed to do or did not have the chance to do. What was at stake was the survival of the creative spirit in inimical circumstances. Lynn fought for creativity.

Fighting was an integral part of Lynn's experience, but her dream was not limited to combat. I tried to protect her dream from invasion by attitudes external to it. One also could relate her dream to sexual themes with oedipal or lesbian elements, since climbing the stairs refers to a heightening of sexual tensions. The structure of the dream sequence included, but ought not be limited to, sexual and aggressive themes. There is a logic to going up, then the appearance of an erection—images of ascension. Lynn and Mary indeed went up. They got higher or, in the vernacular, they got an "up," a "high," a "turn-on" about what they did.

With Mary as a stimulus, Lynn met and enjoyed an aspect of her own active, creative power. She fought for it, but the dream took her beyond fighting and the sense of victimization. In the dream she, Mary, and the erect man simply were. There was the simple existence of upward flow without paranoia or oppression. There might come a time when it would be important to explore hidden determinants of Lynn's provocativeness. At the present juncture, however, what was most important was her *feeling of breakthrough.*

It is no accident that Lynn's fight for creativity, even if through a proxy, came after sessions which dealt with fury and chaos or unintegration. In previous work Lynn allowed herself to become more disorganized and taste the raw flow of affects. She tried to see and feel at the same time. For moments she dropped between the cracks of usual experience and tolerated not being who she thought she was. Now her anger and creative impulse came together, and she fought for what was most important to her.

Deeper Than Sexual Excitement

A week later Lynn began her session by talking about a dream. She scarcely said hello before the dream was out of her mouth. She was letting me in on an ongoing conversation.

> Lynn: "A man, maybe Andy, wanted to tell me something about himself. It was the oddest thing, as if it were not Andy or a man but the dream talking. As if the dream wanted to tell me something about itself but used a figure, a man, to speak through.
>
> "I warned him that my parents were sleeping and might wake up and find out. He said, 'Don't worry about that. I'll fix that.' But I was worried. I was afraid for him to speak. I wanted to stop him from revealing himself and waking them up."

> M.E.: [I appreciated the dream but did not know what to say. I had many questions and thoughts. It was wonderful and strange that the dream allowed Lynn a glimpse of the way it embodies itself in a particular figure. The dream, the man, wanted to reveal something. It-he wanted to reveal it-himself. But self-disclosure meant waking up parents, and this Lynn feared. She protected the dream, the man, and her parents from one another, and herself from them. She did not want to let them meet and take their chances. She feared what would happen. But how was the man going to fix things? What did he want to say? Why was Lynn so afraid of waking her parents?] "It seems like everything got stopped short."

> Lynn: "Stopped short? Well, maybe, yes. Hearing your voice makes me more nervous. Hearing you makes me

anxious. Sexually. I felt—feel—very hot sexually. The harder I tried to stop it, the more it became. Is that what I'm stopping short? This was the hottest week I've had. All these feelings came out toward Andy. I had the hottest, heaviest, most hysterical time. Andy was happy, but I was nervous. At one point he misinterpreted a kind of trance I was in and came quickly, ruining a good thing. It got stopped short and I became nervous. I'm nervous now. Sexually nervous. I don't want to talk about it."

M.E.: "Like you didn't want the man in the dream to talk?"

Lynn: "'I forbid it.' Those are the words that come. 'I forbid it.' Mother would say, 'No, you're too young yet.' I would think, 'I'll have it when—' I feel removed from the whole thing. It's ridiculous."

M.E.: "Who's afraid of waking up?"

Lynn: "According to Andy, something must have happened with me last session. He said I came home and attacked him sexually. I wasn't aware of it. He asked what went on in the session that made the change. He questions me more about therapy after episodes like that. I'm intense in sessions. Andy says he sees a change in my attitude after sessions. He says I'm more attentive to his likes.

"I'm ready. How well I know I'm ready. I remember thinking I'm ready. 'You're not ready yet.' That's what I heard. I heard my father saying that and sending me to mother. I heard mother saying that, and I was alone. On Sundays the three of us [Lynn's brother, sister, and herself] would lie in bed between our parents, watching

TV. I think of that now with a lot of sexy feelings and deeper than sexual feelings. There was the sexiness but also the love, the togetherness—such a deep feeling. I feel like weeping that we had this closeness.

"My mother's voice saying, 'She's not ready yet,' is wounding. She sent me away. I was afraid of what she would say. She was right to forbid me. I was too young. But I could not believe her. She was really saying, 'Do what I say and you'll be happy, like your happy sister.' My sister was happy, happier than I. My sister fought more, but I was angrier. I *am* angrier. My sister demands more, but I'm more demanding. She is easier going. Feelings come and go. I hold on to things. Look at the way I beat out the chairman of my department. I outfoxed him and stayed in there, and my student won the day. I pushed her, backed her. I was pushing her past my mother. I was saying, 'I am ready. We are ready. Let's go, let's do it now.' There's so much to battle. It released so much energy that I went home and fucked my head off. I went crazy. I can't believe how crazy I got. It can go either way. I can go crazy with my body now or get stuck in my head. Both are so intense. I think Andy's a little afraid of me, but he likes it."

M.E.: "He's for being ready?"

Lynn: "In the sexual areas maybe. Maybe in other things, too. I'm not sure. I get the idea he takes me for granted and holds me back. I'm supposed to be there to support him but not do too much myself. But I'm beginning to think I hold myself back. Whenever I do something, he's proud of me. He comes through on my side. Maybe I've been mixing him up with my parents, the voice that says, 'You're not ready yet. Listen to me.' He got turned on when I got turned on. Not only sexually. He was all for me seeing Mary's project through.

87

He's for me taking courses, doing more of the things I want to do. I've been sealed up in myself, not seeing right in some ways. I've been mad at him for holding me back. I wonder how much it's been him or me.

"Maybe Andy's not as bad as I thought. Deep down I always loved him. I see his faults. I think he's great anyway. I love him. In a way it's like the love that made me weepy when I thought of us all in my parents' bed together. If I didn't feel safe with Andy, I couldn't let myself go the way I did. That safety comes from a very deep place. I lose it. But it lets me open up when it comes."

For the moment, Lynn pushed past a barrier. Her vindictiveness toward the chairman of her department paid off. It now became clear that the man was a stand-in for parental authority that made her feel like an incapable or bad child. Perhaps her parents had treated her in an age-appropriate way, but the message that came across was, "Your happiness depends on doing as I say." Lynn learned very early that doing as her parents wished did not make her happy. But doing as she wished did not bring happiness either. It made things difficult.

Lynn saw an opening and seized it. She ran interference for Mary, who symbolized her child self and her creative self. She defeated the ogre, the inhibiting force. Her triumph was followed by a release of sexual energy, a kind of sustained hysterical outburst. In part she used sex to discharge the tension that built up in her conflict at work. However, she had not been so thoroughly sexual before. It seemed that an orderly sequence occurred: Her heightened and focused self-assertion at work was followed by a breakthrough of sexual feelings. *A general heightening of being had consequences in diverse areas of functioning.*

Lynn's self-assertion and sexual excitement swept past normal critical barriers. She also made contact with a dimension she sensed was deeper than self-assertion and sexual excitement: the sense of bonding with her family in childhood. She implied that this bonding acted as the background that made self-assertion and sexual fulfillment possible or profitable. It was the bonding that enabled her to land on her feet and permit what might have been self-destructive to turn into something creative and growth producing. It was this deeper bonding that enabled Lynn to feel safe enough to allow more of her sexuality to emerge with her husband.

The possibility of more gratification with Andy, in turn, was concordant with a revisualization of Andy and herself. Lynn now doubted that he was as great a cause of her holding herself back as she had imagined. She had experienced a breakthrough past her usual boundaries and tasted what she might be capable of doing and feeling. If Andy was frightened, he also liked it. Lynn felt he was on her side. He enjoyed the fruits of her victory.

It was not surprising that within a couple of weeks Lynn, in dialectical fashion, dreamt about her eyes. In this dream she was sitting around a table with colleagues, going over teaching lists. Lynn's list was extended, as if she were being given a vote of confidence. At the same time a man was checking into her sight problem. He was helping Lynn pry her eyes open, little by little. It was hard for her to keep them open.

Lynn already said she had not seen Andy properly. Her dream validated her difficulty with seeing. It also gave expression to her sense of renewal. Not only could Lynn feel more, she also was learning to see more. Seeing and feeling were growing together.

The unknown man in the dream most likely referred to me. But it would have been ungracious to point out that her recent gains came about as a result of the support and challenge of therapy, or that she was enacting in real life various transference elements. In time the pendulum would swing, and we would have to discuss the ins and outs of our relationship again. There was no immediate need to refer her gains to therapy and diminish the pride and pleasure in herself.

The Mouse Gets Bigger

We were now in our third year of work. We had come a long way from the first session in which Lynn mostly talked about her brother's problems and her husband's dislike of therapy. In our years together Lynn tasted rage, terror, emptiness, self-assertion, and heightened sexual excitement. Her work situation was more difficult but more interesting. She took more courses to better her position. Her marriage improved. She could have stopped therapy at this point, but the therapy work had too much momentum. Lynn was becoming increasingly interested in what her psyche would produce next. There seemed to be no end to what could happen. Following are excerpts from sessions in our third year.

Key Stages in Lynn's Therapy

Lynn: "Here I am. I feel I've been seeing you forever. Things keep happening. For a long time I felt whatever happened in therapy just happened in my sessions. Nothing leaked into my life. Then things started happening outside of therapy, and therapy dried up. Now I feel the opposite. Things are happening in therapy again, but my life is not going anywhere. There's always some problem. In a way my problems seem to get bigger the more I'm here.

"I dreamt of a charcoal-grey mouse scurrying around a wall. Andy tried to hit it. It got bigger, the size of a cat. It bit my hand as I tried to hit it. I got a big book to hit it, but it kept biting my hand. It held on, a tenacious grip. I backed away from it but it came after me. I was scared shitless."

M.E.: "You were just talking about therapy's bite."

Lynn: "Yes. My problems look bigger, not smaller, the more I'm here. You'd think I'd get better. I didn't think I had so many problems when I came here. Now I don't see any end to them. Will I ever get out of here?"

M.E: [After Lynn exhausted therapy as a theme, I shifted ground.] "Do you know anyone who uses the mouth as a weapon?"

Lynn: "You don't mean me, Miss Loud Mouth? I know I have a mouth. But I don't see myself that way. I speak up for myself. No one's going to get away with things. But inside I'm a mouse. I'm scared and sensitive. I get hurt easily. But I refuse to get bullied. You won't shut me up easily. I'm not going to give in to myself. I won't cave in."

It was true that Lynn remained something of a loud mouth. It bothered me at times. I could feel shut out and

91

ssaulted when her barrage of words started, often strings of complaints. She could not let up once she started. What bothered me more than the complaints was the brittle, machinegun quality of her barrage. Often she could not let go of a hurt until she changed the hurtful reality in some way. This might be futile in many cases, but sometimes she got results.

> Lynn: "I know I can be biting, but I don't feel that way. I used to think of myself more like a tiny, helpless mouse. But this mouse isn't so helpless. It's a terror. Is that the way my mother experienced me when I came at her as a baby? Was she afraid of me? I'm afraid of myself. But I won't let go. I won't let go of you and you won't let go of me. Therapy sticks to me and I stick to it. I used to feel Andy wouldn't let go either. I'd look down at Andy for his needs. I looked down at my father for hiding his needs. My mouse doesn't let go. It demands attention. It makes sure I notice it. I have to deal with it.
>
> "It's not just scary. It feels disgusting. I want to disown it. Like my crazy mind or sexual feelings. They go out of control, and I don't think they're me. I don't feel me in them when I go crazy. I can see this mouse is part of me, but I can't feel it is part of me now. I don't want it to be me. I want it to disappear, to go back in its hole."

> M.E.: "Was there a hole in the dream?"

> Lynn: "No, not in the dream. But now I think of a hole for the mouse to hide in. I guess it's been hiding."

> M.E.: "What's the hole like?"

Key Stages in Lynn's Therapy

Lynn: "I know what you're thinking. Analysts think alike. You all think about one thing."

M.E.: "Try to visualize *this* hole."

Lynn: "I start to think that you're thinking about my vagina. But what I see is a hole with a lot of shit stuffed in it. I can't make out what the shit is."

M.E.: "Maybe part of your crazy mind and sexual feelings are stuffed in there. Or maybe my therapy madness, therapy shit."

Lynn: "I'm afraid to let go. All that shit will come out. If this mouse was in there, imagine what else I'll find. I want to pinch tight and hold the rest in. The mouse is scary enough. I don't want to see any more."

M.E.: "You've been saying for three years how some baby part of you was made to feel shitty."

Lynn: "I try to hide it. I've always been more constipated than my sister. All this holding back and going blank. Then the words running out of my mouth. A diarrhea of the mouth. I know that. I know I'm a loud mouth. I know I bad-mouth people. I know I run off at my mouth. I can be mean. But I don't feel mean. I feel like I can't hurt anyone. I feel hurt, but I don't believe my words can hurt. I feel I'm just protecting myself. I hit the mouse with all my might, and it kept coming. It didn't even feel my hitting it. It didn't slow down a bit. It just kept coming. Its bite has power, but I have no power. I hit and hit and nothing happens. That's a good reason for blanking out."

93

M.E.: "Often the best you could do was blank out. It's not your fault. No one taught you how to work with the mouse. No one helped you with *this* mouse. You say your mother was frightened by it. She couldn't handle it. She tried to make it go away, to brainwash it, to hide it. In therapy that doesn't work. Everything comes out. Now this mouse is out. We have a chance to find out how to work with it. You couldn't do it alone. It turned against you. You tried to disown it, and it wouldn't let go. The more you tried to kill it, the bigger it got. We will see what you can do with it with some help."

The next week Lynn said she felt grateful for this session. She left feeling just right, not too empty or filled. Feeling just the right balance was rare for her, and so were expressions of gratitude. Her good feeling lasted nearly two weeks, until a dream threatened to make her feel badly.

The Freezer

Lynn: "I've been feeling really good these past weeks, ever since the mouse session. What a relief. I've been so much freer. Now I'm afraid something's wrong again. It's hard to take the idea that there's always going to be something wrong. I'd like life always to be the way it's been these past couple of weeks. I'd like to think that someday most of my life will be like that. But as long as I'm here it seems to be one disturbance after another."

I thought of asking if her disturbances were because of therapy, but then thought that Lynn was using therapy to organize her sense of disturbance. What a luxurious relief to use therapy as a magnet for drawing out problems!

Lynn: "I dreamt somebody delivered a refrigerator with something wrong with the freezer compartment. Andy and I plugged it in and stocked it with food. The next time we opened the refrigerator, there was a crack in the seam and liquid poured down the back of the refrigerator. It began to flood. The water on the bottom got higher. The man who brought it couldn't understand that something was wrong. His own refrigerator worked fine."

M.E.: "Do you remember your first dream in therapy? Your house was on fire. Now your freezer doesn't work."

Lynn: "I run hot and cold. I'm hotheaded with my bosses. I get furious with Andy and my parents, but cold, too. Sometimes when I get the hots Andy is frightened but likes it. He hates when I'm frozen, but he's more patient now. I give him the silent treatment or run off at the mouth. It's hard to find a balance. Too hot or too cold."

M.E.: "In the dream the freezer is cracked. Something's wrong with the container. Perhaps you feel I'm not sympathetic enough."

Lynn: "You let me run on. You don't do enough. Maybe you're not strong enough for me. You can't hold everything I put into you."

M.E.: "I should help you cool off and take care of what's too hot to handle. Or warm you up and help you thaw out of your deep freeze. I ought to be a better thermo-stat or mood regulator."

Lynn: "I'll be seeing you forever unless I regulate my own temperature. I do better but not as well as I'd like. Do you know I feel these things physically? I shiver when I feel too hot or too cold. I actually freeze and burn up. Andy is more even. I'm hysterical."

M.E.: "You have a wider range of feeling than Andy?"

Lynn: "Yes. But his feelings run very deep. Mine run through my skin."

M.E.: "The skin of the refrigerator is very hard."

Lynn: "I go back and forth between this metallic hard-ness and being totally thin-skinned."

M.E.: "In the dream the compartment that's faulty is on top. So different from the fire in the basement."

Lynn: "You mean the fire is down below and the cool-ing is up above?"

M.E.: "Is that the way you've ordered it? Is that the basic order?"

Lynn became thoughtful, and the session ended peacefully. I felt we had gotten to something basic. In the session, Lynn rehearsed her hot-cold fluctuations. She went over ways she heated up and froze. A basic order became clearer.

I suggested she might be criticizing me for being cracked, too cold, or for not being a good enough container (either actually or as father and mother transference elements). She agreed, but we did not take this far. The focus turned back on herself. Perhaps I deflected her criticism, perhaps she was afraid of being too dependent on me, or perhaps Lynn's drive for autonomy asserted itself. Whatever the case, Lynn's longing to take the bull by the horns won out. She felt a deficit and longed for a remedy: she wanted her own good ventilating system.

As she turned over her feelings, I brought together her dream images of burning and freezing, the ancient elements of fire and ice. Her unconscious was sorting things out. Perhaps it is too simple to associate heat with passion and coolness with head. For Lynn fire and ice were also mixed in body experience. She could be hot-headed and icy-hearted. She showed a variety of top-bottom/hot-cold mixtures. Nevertheless, what once seemed to be mute, kaleidoscopic arrays of changing states ripping her apart now seemed part of implicitly meaningful and patterned, if exquisitely amorphous, flows.

The Paternal Pivot

Most of Lynn's anger throughout our several years together was directed at her mother and husband, then her bosses, and, finally, her brother, father, and me. She linked her basic personality problems with her mother and only secondarily with her father. Her mother was the loud, dominant, insensitive, and controlling parent. She did the brainwashing and most of the communicating. Lynn felt tied up with her mother's energy, goodwill, demandingness, and possessive love.

Lynn felt she owed her life to her mother. At least her mother was active and alive and interactive, even if on her own terms. Lynn believed that she withdrew and tightened up in the face of her mother's blindness. She became paralyzed in response to her mother's attempt to take her over and treat her like a satellite. Yet her activity level was more like her mother's than her father's. In some way she froze, but in another she became like her mother. She could do things with seemingly endless energy, while feeling profoundly inhibited. Lynn spent a good deal of time trying to get her mother to respond to her as she really was. She tried to remove her mother's blinders, soften her insensitivity, and burst the egocentric bubble that hindered real intimacy.

Nevertheless, in the weeks after the freezer dream her father took center stage in therapy. He had been the focus before but not so intensely. She had voiced anger at him for not asserting himself in the family. He took a quiet backseat and let his wife fill the vacuum. Lynn wished he would have protected her and balanced things out.

She made excuses for him. Perhaps her mother would not give him space and was too much for him. Perhaps it was not mainly his fault. Still it bothered Lynn. She was furious at him for being ill. She believed his bad heart was linked to his personal weakness. If he could stand up for himself and not let his wife be so bossy, he might be healthier.

Key Stages in Lynn's Therapy

What went on in him? Did he suffer? Was he blank? Was he the cause of her vacuum? She wished she could tell what he was like inside.

Lynn: "The oddest thing is that I can't stand it when he talks. When he finally says something, I turn off. I can't listen to him. I feel raped by his words, by the very sound of his voice. Why should this be? I know other people who have nothing to say. I can at least be polite. I pretend to listen. I respond nicely. But I can't do that with him. I tell myself, 'Next time I'll be nicer. I'll sit and listen. I'll talk.' But when the time comes I can't get away fast enough. I want to scream at him, 'Shut up, Daddy!'

"When he just sits I sense his love, even though he's so pathetic. He looks done in, yet warm. I can at least weave a fantasy of goodness around him. But as soon as he opens his mouth it's like chalk squeaking on a blackboard. When I was a kid I used to get a lot of ear infections. Now I think it was because of the way he spoke. I used to think I had to shut my mother out. But she I listen to. She makes me furious, but I hear her. I know what she's like inside. I don't give my father a chance. I'm afraid he's a swamp, and I'll get sucked in. He's some kind of amorphous, yucky monster—no form, no insight, no verve.

"I'm unfair, I know. I can't help it. I've got to say how I feel. Maybe I'm talking about something yucky and despairing about myself. But I didn't get it from my mother. She doesn't have those kinds of feelings. I got them from him. I want to fight him now. I see him yelling at me. He's yelling at me with all his might. He never yelled that way. Or did he? He had outbursts. I remember his rages. I'd stare at him. I'd shut off and stare. That would make him madder. He wasn't so nice. I had

99

contempt for him because he had no better way to communicate. He spoke in platitudes, placating, or bossy. You couldn't take his orders seriously, and he'd be reduced to helpless fits.

"Now I picture him yelling and yelling. Maybe I wish he'd let go and get it all out. Maybe I want him to outscream me. Maybe he is my scream. I feel relief when he screams. I don't want him to stop. I don't want him to lose. Yet I stare at him coldly and am bound to win. My ear is aching. My chest is aching. I numb off but stare with hatred. Here is where I become frigid. I'm getting tense. Can you imagine? I want to suck his cock. I want to do it right. I want to have the perfect feeling. I don't want to feel too stuffed and choked or too empty. Taking his penis the right way makes me feel right. It balances things off.

"You see? I've given him a penis. I've forced it on him. I've turned his rage into something I can use, something I need. I can't bear to hear him but am finding a way to take him in. I've tensed up to keep him out. Now I can feel myself relaxing.

"I think I always hear my father yelling at me without knowing it. Tension builds without my being aware of it. When I'm aware of it, I don't know why it's there. He's yelling inside me. I never heard him inside me that way before. If I did, I didn't know what I was hearing. I didn't know there was anything to hear. Now I feel that his raging scream is always going on and tense up to shield myself, so as not to hear it. I freeze and squeeze myself tight and blot myself out to blot *it* out. I didn't realize how tightly I hold myself. I'm all squeezed up.

"I want to relax and let him in. My body can take it. I'm easily annoyed and irritated, an impatient person. I'm high-strung. I don't want to fall into his morass, his swamp. I don't want to be raped by his rage and self-pity. I get more and more annoyed seeing the shutting-out. I get furious that I have to close myself off. I want to make myself stay open and take it and get over it. I'm sure this is why I get my back and chest pains, my earaches, my vaginal infections. I physicalize in all sorts of little, annoying ways. I'm practically never free of something that bothers me."

M.E.: "You can practice opening little by little."

Lynn: "I know. I'm going to. I'm doing it. I'm furious. If I don't do something more, I'll be more furious."

When the session ended, I felt that something decisive had occurred. An inner world with Lynn's father as center was evolving. Up until now her mother had been at the core of Lynn's sense of what was wrong. Now she would have two centers of sickness and health to struggle with. One could expect a more differentiated reading of her life to develop. Lynn would have two internal baby tyrants in search of a biography, in search of growth. This increase in complexity might make life harder, but the internal division of labor implied by a stronger inner couple might also bring more freedom.

"I Want a Baby"

After the weekend, Lynn said she felt good. She didn't physicalize all weekend. She said she had something to tell me, then launched into a dream she had Saturday night.

Lynn: "Andy and I were in Washington, D.C., with another couple, Lois and Art. We were touring. Andy, Lois, and Art met to eat. There was an odd moment when they were doing something like playing musical chairs for the tables. I was separate. Andy ran over to me to tell me that Lois was in labor in the back room. Another couple was there with the woman in labor, too. Lois put her head on Andy's lap. The other woman's head was on her husband's lap. She was undressed from the waist down. The baby was coming two months early. The woman was in a birthing position with her legs up, like a baby herself." [After a long pause] "Can you guess what I want to tell you?"

M.E.: "You're pregnant?"

Lynn: [Laughs] "No. I want to have a baby. I really do. I never dreamt of having a baby before. I've had enough to handle without a baby. But I want one. I'm scared of really doing it but I want to."

M.E.: "That's terrific."

Lynn: "It was a crazy dream—all the running around chairs and tables. Confusing. I understand that I want to have a baby, but I don't understand anything else about it."

M.E.: "Maybe the running around is a kind of sexual movement. It came before the babies."

Lynn: "Why was everyone else doing it and not me?"

M.E.: "I don't know. But in your last session you went further in getting a stronger inner couple, mother *and* father. Maybe they had intercourse since we saw each other last."

Lynn: "I can tear that down, but I know what you mean. The restaurant scene is like sex in a way. Sex is a kind of eating, nourishment. Everyone seems to be playing, having fun. A kind of playground. That's a nice way to have sex. I never pictured my parents doing it that way."

M.E.: "Maybe the parents inside you are getting a little better."

Lynn: "Two couples are having babies."

M.E.: [Lynn paused. She wanted me to say something. I could ask questions or extrapolate about the meaning of foursome, symbol of psychic unity. Freud wrote about the multiplicity within the internal couple (see Meltzer, 1973, 1977; Eigen, 1974). My more immediate concern was with Lynn's joy and fear. She needed a response, not analytic formality.] "Maybe your dream is trying to drive home the message that birth is possible. Two women are doing it and it's okay. You need to see it's possible because you're so scared."

Lynn: "But the baby is coming too soon."

M.E.: "Am I rushing you?"

Lynn: "No. You're echoing me. It's me who's rushing. Only I can't say I've rushed. I've waited. I've been putting it off."

M.E.: "Maybe it feels like the only way you'll do it is by rushing ahead."

Lynn: "If I wait until I'm ready, I'll never do it. I can spend my life waiting until I'm ready. My sister did it and I envied her, but it wasn't right for me. Now it's getting time. I don't have to be like her. She's so natural, softer than I am. I would look at her with Josh and think I could never be like her. I could never be as good a mother. Now I feel we don't have to be the same. Maybe that's why there are two or three couples. Each is different. Something the same, something different. If they can do it, so can I."

In dreams, duplications may represent intensity. That there were three couples in the restaurant, and two women in labor, indicates that Lynn was dealing with very strong emotions. Why was she seemingly left out? In what way was she left out?

That she was more aloof than the others reflects an aspect of her personality, a sense of inferiority-superiority that goes along with a sense of exclusion, a distancing operation. The child experiences itself as excluded from parental sexual activity and is often consigned to being an onlooker. Now that the father image was important enough to make a stronger parental couple, Lynn's sense of being left out became more serious.

At the same time her appreciation of the birth process increased. She participated by proxy. She watched safely from a distance, but it was also herself she was watching. It was as if she doubled or tripled in order to test out what it might be like to give birth. It was of inestimable importance that an image of birthing could appear in a dream. It referred to her therapy birth, the long process of being reborn through therapy. But it also referred to the physical process of gestation and birth and the fears involved. Lynn was beginning to practice giving birth. That she did this in a dream shows she was enacting her wish and fears very deeply. She was taking time to prepare.

It was no accident that her desire to have a baby surfaced after her father became more central. Did this mean she hoped to have her father's baby but was afraid to? If so, having babies would be taboo or an act of defiance. Perhaps a deficient father image spoiled her sense of impregnation and birth; a shift in father image changed the way fertilization, gestation, and birth felt. In the preceding session she had fought to let her father in. She was determined to get over disgust with paternal deficiencies. She did not want to shut her other out. She vowed to stay open no matter what.

Her attitude paid off. The dream combined observation with action. Lynn saw the supportive, nurturant aspect of males. She saw that birth was real. In some way she had not believed in birth or that she could live through it. She would have to do it herself, but her dream left room for seeing and doing and the help of others. She was both alone and with others who had the same experiences she did. The image of birth represented her more open attitude.

Why Washington, D.C.? I do not know why the dream picked this way of representing something of capital importance. The image of birth expressed growth of structure and generativity. Lynn's psyche mirrored its own renewal.

The End of Therapy

Lynn's therapy ended when she had a child, nearly three years after the session just described. I suspect more patients begin, rather than end, therapy with the birth of a child. I felt Lynn ought to stay in therapy, that in many ways she was just beginning.

I would be more understanding today, now that I have children of my own. Lynn continued to see me for several months after she had her little girl. I don't think I really heard her when she spoke of what a bother it was to come to see me. She was absorbed in taking care of her baby. She had to drive nearly an hour to get to my office. She did not have time for me. She did not want to break her new rhythm. Therapy was in another world; she was somewhere else.

For me, psyche was all. What did I know of babies? I had read D. W. Winnicott, who spoke expressively about the mother-infant tie. I *knew* about the importance of early mothering. I lived it *imaginatively*. But the *actual* experience was something else. To me it sounded as if Lynn were making excuses.

In retrospect, I am amazed she stuck it out with me as long as she did. She had to break away from my not wanting to let go. I give her credit for leaving, as well as for seeing me. I was fixed more on where she was stuck than on how far she had come.

I was troubled by a block reinforced by Lynn's work situation. The strident way she spoke about teaching did not change. She fought with students as well as superiors. So many students tried to get away without working; there were so many discipline problems. Teaching was policing. Lynn managed to rescue a sense of creativeness in hostile and oppressive circumstances, but the price was high.

It bothered me that chronic combativeness tied her up. Her existence seemed to be a stream of complaints and obsessions about daily injuries and obstacles. She bad-mouthed villains and primed herself for battle. I formed the impression (for which I now feel apologetic) that teaching high school kept her personality small. So much energy spent guarding her position, gearing for combat! Her work problems seemed to justify the need for a defensive personality.

Lynn spoke about her wish to do something else, but nothing she thought of offered financial security. She was in her thirties, and each year brought her closer to retirement and a pension. By the time she was forty she would have twenty years in. She had too much to lose by leaving. She would stick it out. She hated it. She loved it. It was her life.

Motherhood was her life. Her marriage was her life. Teaching was her life. She loved art and photography. Lynn was not as I wished her to be, but she was living her own life.

I think of the tightness in her face and voice, which more therapy may have helped. But I also think of her brightness and verve and aliveness. She followed her heart's promptings. She was a mixture of moxie and sensitivity, a street fighter in love with creativeness.

I don't blame myself for wanting her to stay. I think back to our first session. What if I had not taken her?

What if I had gone along with her style of dismissing her problems? She would have gotten by with pluck and determination, as most people do. But how much she would have missed! How much more she found within herself, her life, her family! It was not farfetched for me to think that more investment would pay greater dividends.

When I reflected on my regret at Lynn's decision, I saw in myself something I had seen in her throughout our work—an image of my face as pinched, maligned, irritated, with a twinge of self-pity. Was my failure to admit twinship with her the reason she was rejecting me? Had she deposited in me a contracted aspect of herself? Was she rejecting me or simply going on with her own life? Did I inherit the blend of sensitivity and anger that characterized her these many years?

I watched the sensitive, angry image of myself until my vision blurred and broke into a smile. My inner image also smiled and grew bigger, then stopped smiling and grew smaller. When it was small, it looked frightened, accusing, pained, guarded, and longing. My real face continued to smile while I watched the inner image contract and expand. My chest contracted and expanded with it, my heart a beating soul.

I thought of Lynn's face. By the end of therapy her face could go through enormous changes in a brief time, very like my soul's face within. She could be white and small, then vivid, warm, and filled out. Her feelings could shift from fear to happiness in moments, back and forth repeatedly. How life-giving these changes felt! Often she felt joy at the center of shifting currents, safely suspended in a clear, still point.

My own contracting-expanding self mirrored one of Lynn's principal achievements: her increased ability to tolerate movements between a smaller and bigger I as they struggled to be partners. Perhaps she came to therapy to discover that these movements were real and part of what makes life worth living.

Chapter Four

Self-Other

The Self-Other Context

Self and other constitute each other. There is no other without self, no self without other.[1] This is a premise that permeates all my therapy work and writings. I do not and cannot define these terms. They are open. With each individual and each session, I have a chance to learn anew what self and other can be.

No two therapy sessions are the same. This is like saying you can't step into the same river twice. It is also true that you can never step out of the river. Self-other is the medium we live in—our emotional river, our psychological air, our matrix. Our moods and attitudes, the flavor of our lives feed and are fed by changing nuances and intensities of self-other dramas.

We fight our selves, each other, our times. We war against limitations, defects, injustices. The might of the

---

[1]With variations, this view is shared by many workers from diverse fields, e.g., Buber (1958), Luijpen (1960), Kohut (1971), Elkin (1972), Lacan (1977), and Stern (1977).

warrior and the ecstasy of power are exhilarating, but they ebb and flow. A time comes for the mighty to run and hide, to be clever, patient, and learn the lessons of weakness. Strong now, weak later; weak now, strong later. The wheel turns. Self and other redistribute themselves along variable axes of power.

The wounded, dying God-man who rises again—that is our daily story. We die and are reborn through wounds every day. We are planted in our wounds; we rise above them. The soil of our lives is fertilized by our deaths, yet we are also new. We keep trying to get it right: a better death, a better rebirth.

Creativity, love, power can be cruel. We seek moments of radiant completeness and are blown away when we encounter radiance in the guise of pure, raw power, even when it is destructive, horrifying, disgusting. There is no radiance that is not embedded in some kind of self-other context, if only in fantasy. We must learn to explore types of self-other channels that create flows of radiance which affirm, rather than menace, life. We must search out ways to foster genuinely freeing mutuality.

Therapy is an experiment in mutuality. This sounds odd because therapy is centered on one person, the client, who is enjoined to reveal all while the therapist remains hidden. There is much that can be said about the asymmetry of power in the therapy relationship. The therapist can satisfy all kinds of power and safety needs at the patient's expense. The patient can also make the therapist pay. Therapy is not an easy business, and the therapist is as much slave as master, subject to patient whims, manipulations, veiled threats, emotional and financial blackmail. One of the main jobs of the therapy couple is to process what is wrong with the therapy relationship.

Mutuality in therapy is deeper than surface imbalances. The therapist nurses the patient's private and hidden impact. The affective impact of the patient gives rise to thoughts and feelings that the therapist lives with and eventually finds ways of using. Selections are made that stimulate processing ability in the patient. Therapy provides opportunities for re-processing experience. Resonance goes on from processor to processor.

Patient and therapist gradually learn how to be with each other. They continuously process what goes on between them. They learn how to get along with and make use of each other's personalities in ways that are freeing. Processing ability may catch up with and grow beyond "off points." What is wrong may or may not be correctable, but one can grow in the knowledge of what is wrong. Processing ability may not dissolve or change what is wrong so much as develop contexts that re-situate it, take it into account, at times move beyond it.

In the therapy context, ruptures and chronic deformations of self-other relatedness are given a chance to play themselves out in a self-other context that keeps growing. When things go sufficiently well, the therapy relationship is not destroyed or permanently marred by what would break down or deform ordinary personal and business relationships. Therapy absorbs the toxins and warps and works with them. One grows in ability to process disabilities and malignancies that spoil life's possibilities. Infinitesimal increments of growth in processing ability can make an infinite difference.

Les's Grapples with Self-Other

Les was at war with his mother Bess, but for many years he hoped the war would blow over without having to fight. It was a long, silent war. For Les, his mother was an engulfing presence. She made Les feel that she and he truly understood each other, that they had a special bond. She permeated his insides.

From her special home inside him, Bess directed Les's life. Like a good master, she gave Les areas of freedom. She dictated life in ways that gave him pleasure. Rebellion seemed inimical to his interests. He had a good job, a family he loved. His gut feeling was that he owed it all to Bess; if he rebelled, everything would vanish, like making a wrong move in a fairy tale.

Yet Les had a will to be free, to be his own boss. He wanted to break out of his shell and live the life he knew was in him. Closeness with his mother also empowered him. He knew love existed, even if egoism and neediness strangled it. Les was also a free spirit, a romantic impaled on a pattern. Throughout his marriage, he and his wife impulsively took off for short, passionate trips. Business did not have the last word. He was dissatisfied with the materialism in which he was trapped. He wanted something of his own, something he created. He rebelled against his upbringing. The type of specialness his mother inculcated made it impossible for him to settle for what she wanted. To be a cog in a machine did not give him the feeling of specialness he needed.

His mother's threats of abandonment heightened his sensitivity. All his life anxiety bit him. Fears and failings tortured him and made him ashamed of himself. He needed to do more, to be more. Throughout his life, Les gathered courage for the fight that mattered.

Les's father was in the background. He never inwardly gave up, although outwardly he abandoned the family to Bess. Les's father was not simply absent; he was someone who *might* be there. He wished his children well and played with them. He took them to Little League games, like Les did with his own boys. There was always the promise that something more *might* happen. Even near the end of therapy, Les hoped his father might yet play a greater role in his life.

His father's voice was a background voice of discontent, a voice that waited, bided time. It taught Les patience; his turn would come in the long run. His father's failure gave Les space. His father was more peaceful than his mother. He did not fill time with engulfment/ intrusion/abandonment anxieties. Les's mother kept him busy with the states she put him through. His father was less demanding. He wanted to play with his children or be left in peace. From his father, Les learned that people could enjoy one another for the fun of it, and leave one another alone. Les's father and mother combined to form an inner couple that was not at peace. Father and mother within him were a constant source of turmoil. Both valued family; both were unhappy in family life. They did not want to be together. They did not even like each other. How could discord not be a part of Les's marriage? It is a tribute to the human heart, and the hearts of his parents, that love won.

Les came to therapy for something more than mere survival. If he were not to be miserable for his entire life, he needed to do something more than his parents in working with the diverse pulls of his being. The give-and-take of therapy sessions provided a focus for currents that ripped him apart.

Coming Together

Les tried to win me over by being a "good boy." He threw himself into therapy with the same energy and determination with which he made business deals. To an extent, this worked. He got new insights and pushed himself to improve. But therapy could not be controlled. He then punished me by being a "bad boy," by coming late and missing sessions. He also became angry at my inability to do better.

Les was furious with his mother for the mixture of seduction, control, and abandonment that characterized her behavior. He was furious at me because I was not sufficiently seductive and controlling. I maintained a friendly, therapeutic distance but was not abandoning.

Les was angry at his father for not playing more of a role in his life. He was angry at me for not doing more. I bounced back from streams of accusations that Les feared would kill his father off. Les had never spoken himself out so thoroughly before, not in a situation that could handle it.

His parents loved Les as I never could. Yet therapy offered a relationship in which Les tolerated and worked with the gaps, deficits, and destructiveness of his most intimate relationships. In therapy Les communicated emotions aroused and short-circuited by those closest to him. He always wanted to acknowledge his own experience of life as fully as possible. In therapy Les's own experiencing was given voice. He began to hear himself.

In circumscribed ways, Les duplicated his parents' behavior. He was controlling, seductive, abandoning, or circuitous vis-à-vis my attempt to maintain a distance-closeness balance that he was not used to. It was as if the worst in his parents reared up in Les to break down the different self-other framework therapy created.

In a way, I was little Les by proxy. He tried to do to me what his parents did to him. We constituted a kind of miniature replica of what went wrong with his life. Roles would shift. If I became seductive-abandoning or resigned, Les could act the innocent victim and triumphantly point his finger. If I became "healthy" again, Les could try to break me down.

With therapy as a context, Les could redirect his fighting spirit, tear away from his mother, face devils in himself, and stand up to weakness. He could say what kind of life he'd like to try to live. Les did not slow down or drop out of being in sessions. He kept moving. But in therapy a different sort of other was the backdrop for his movement. Les gathered himself to fight, hide and run in his usual ways. But instead of the other who loved manipulation, subterfuge, and control, he found the other who loved to hear the truth about life.

I also think it was unusual for Les to find an environment that included patience as an essential ingredient. His impatient personality was built around impatient others who fed on fast reactions. The gap created by therapy exerted a different sort of pressure. Les kept moving along truth gradients. His psychic bones began straightening out. Les could beat Neville the Devil because the therapy context transcended Neville.

One of the breathtaking things about therapy is how a new couple develops in a psychic cesspool. Two people mired in flaws and deficits are uplifted by working through problems together. Week after week we grind out bits and pieces of a bigger picture and grow through the muck. An objective, caring duo is established at the heart of intersubjectivity.

We have moments of feeling free together, then something wrong sticks to us. Sometimes the new therapy couple can rework what is wrong. Sometimes better aspects develop to balance what is wrong. Our vision of our makeup changes. We know what it feels like to come through ourselves. We know we are more than the sum of what is wrong. We are more than the sum of our successes and failures, more than the sum of our capacities. The therapy couple becomes a model of living through the worst together. We move through self and other more deeply into life.

Lynn's Explorations into Self-Other

Whatever felt askew in Lynn's life she displaced onto others. Everyone in her life had maddening faults: brother, mother, father, husband, bosses. Only some of her students were blameless. One student, especially, became a symbol of the innocent, creative, maligned self. Lynn blasted a path through school rules so that the creative self might triumph. The other was "cause" of life's ills but also the carrier of creativity.

Lynn left therapy soon after having a baby. Once again, the other was the carrier of life. Lynn lived through her baby. Nevertheless, Lynn was more fully alive than ever. *She* carried the baby. *She* gave birth. *She* took care of the baby. All this could have happened automatically. Yet Lynn threw herself into her experience fully. She carried her body, and her body carried her. *She* rejoiced, worried, cared, and busied herself with what had to be done. *She* had to deal with work, motherhood, and marriage, as well as say yes-no to the aliveness of her life.

For years, rage had allowed her aliveness to thrive: rage at father for eating/sitting himself to death; rage at mother for her overbearing, good-willed obtuseness; rage at husband for naively wanting everything his way and being so nice about it; rage at bosses for narrowness of vision; rage at herself for not being herself.

Lynn did not leave therapy to get ahead at work, create art, or expand social horizons. She still lived through the other and did most of the things she did before therapy. Nevertheless, the change was enormous.

She tasted herself. She began to thaw out. Lynn spread through her being and had a baby. Salvation was meeting each moment with all that was in her. Little things counted for Lynn, and she poured herself into them. We both felt very proud of what she accomplished.

The Wordless Self

Lynn was a very verbal person, rarely at a loss for words. She spent her days talking to everyone. In therapy words came harder. So much of her talk was complaining and blaming, getting rid of whatever bothered her at the moment. When she tried to locate herself more deeply, she went blank.

In important ways Lynn felt helpless. Her sense of helplessness, in part, derived from her inability to change the behavior and personality of significant people in her life. Her father remained mired in inert, self-destructive behavior; her mother obstinately remained thin-skinned, hysterical, guilt-inducing; her brother kept getting into trouble; her husband remained preoccupied with studies and career. In spite of all her efforts, everyone basically remained the same.

Lynn was thrown back to states akin to the helplessness of childhood. Her parents, as well as she, were helpless in the face of emotions. Her mother externalized and oversimplified emotional life, blasting emotions through a loudspeaker in a global and raw manner. Her father, on the other hand, toned emotions down and even shut them off. For years Lynn filtered her emotional life through her mother's loudspeaker and her father's soundproofing. The ability to let feelings spread and develop was alien.

Lynn went blank in the face of experience, a luxury she had not allowed herself before therapy. If blankness came, she ran from it as fast as possible. Lynn was used to talking her way out of things. She was a very busy person. Her rush of words in therapy covered paralysis and incapacity. She squirmed in her wordlessness. Much of the time emptiness was torture. I took time to get used to it, work with it, appreciate it. In time she acquired more of a taste for the dreaded emptiness. In emptiness, awareness of feelings could develop. In emptiness she was free.

Lynn rarely paused or took a moment before responding. She did not wait to see that she might feel. She tended to meet situations with quick responses, defensive and accusing. The very truth of her perceptions short-circuited growth.

Being right can be as unproductive as being unable to contribute. Having nothing to say may be slavish, while always saying something can be tyrannical, and vice versa. Lynn's fall into emptiness brought her to a place where she was unable to say anything. Her speechlessness came about not simply because she had nothing to say, but because she had gotten to a place where right and wrong did not matter—where it was more important to be than to be right.

Lynn's inability to experience undercut defensive reactions. This was not a defensive paralysis, where one plays dead in hope that the enemy will pass. In Lynn's case what passed by (after husband, brother, father, mother, bosses) was herself, her own burdensome personality, the tangle of quick reactions that imprisoned her, and her own mystery.

Lynn got to a blank spot where massive dissociations between words and experience begin. For Lynn, words were tools for being right rather than ways of communicating experience as fully as possible. Words can stimulate and explore experience, or they can block and freeze and fly so high above experience that connection between verbal and nonverbal dimensions becomes remote. The link between words and experience is never entirely broken, or the gap between them entirely closed. Individuals do their best to play connection and gap against each other.

Lynn went to a wordless spot where realignment between words and experience could occur. She found a zero place of thought and emotions where thinking-feeling-speaking arise together, and she could arise with them. She reached beyond the faults of others and her word machine.

She reached a place where self and silence are utterly alien, utterly intimate. Lynn was reborn through the otherness of the silent self. In this new, blank otherness, there was room for oddity, uncertainty, waiting, and caring. Contacting the mysterious otherness of her most intimate self made her more caring.

Such deep desire lies buried in duty, such fulfillment in caretaking. Lynn did not take care of her baby only because she had to. Being with her baby felt right to her: to feel right rather than be right—a hairsbreadth shift. It felt right to care for her baby, her husband, her father, mother, sister, brother, work, friends. It felt right to care, to throw herself into the ups and downs of every-day living.

The same people and situations that trapped her made her real, deep, and meaningful. In her traps she could use herself fully. She was grateful they were there, all of them, for her to pour herself into. She needed her traps; her emptiness needed them. They filled emptiness and intensified it. She needed activity and emptiness to care for herself. It felt right to care for herself, to fill herself with emptiness, to burst with beautiful moments, to keep on fighting and caring. She was grateful for her small, busy life. There was nothing better for her outside it. It was inexhaustible.

The Endlessness of Self-Other

We do not know where self leaves off and other begins. The very notions of self and other are problematic. The otherness of self is proverbial. Nothing may seem stranger than our selves. Freud and Jung wrote volumes describing aspects of this strangeness. They reveled in the multiplicity of others that make up the self.

Lynn touched the otherness of self when she fell into emptiness and came face to face with her own mysteri-ousness. She kept herself familiar by battling others. At the point where words failed her, a new sense of self opened. She met herself as a stranger. She battled this stranger, too, but the emptiness absorbed her fighting.

She could not fill or exhaust the emptiness inside her. She discovered something in herself bigger than battles.

Les's growth images were more heroic and active. He went on journeys, fought battles. He met and surmounted his own and his other's destructiveness. He pit himself against the worst that was in him and grew in the struggle.

It would be unfair to say that Lynn was passive and Les active. Both were passive, both active. Both were fighters. Both liked good living. But Lynn's therapeutic journey took her into emptiness, whereas Les's took him into destructiveness. Emptiness was *other* for Lynn; destructiveness was *other* for Les. Both grappled with what they most feared.

I doubt if this was simply a male-female difference: males struggle with emptiness, females with destructiveness. No simple gender schema covers the territory, although male-female elements may play a role. One important factor was that Les had children and feared for their safety. Lynn wanted children and made use of therapy to work up the courage to become a mother. In this regard, they were at different points in their lives. They were about the same age, but their tasks were different.

What kind of other was therapy? For both Les and Lynn therapy functioned as a kind of supportive, background other that allowed each to make use of therapy in his or her own way. Les and Lynn spontaneously generated very different therapies with the same therapist. Each crystallized specific constellations of experiences needed to move on, to open, to reshape their lives.

It is impossible to do the therapy experience justice. Obviously a therapist is not a blank screen. Therapy is a very personal business, and personality obtrudes in all kinds of ways. Therapy is a passion, and being a therapist has an ecstatic element. Yet I do empty myself out with each person and try to begin each session new.

I could not predict Lynn's descent into emptiness or Les's battle with Neville the Devil. I could not predict what region of being each would contact and rework or be reworked through. In this sense, a kind of blankness in the therapist allows choice of possibilities. Yet I used my thoughts and feelings and tried this and that blend of silence and speaking. I enjoyed creative use of myself. What a paradoxical situation: to empty out and have fun with what comes. If things go the wrong way, therapy can be horrifying. What an awful thing to see life waste away! But therapy can be great fun, too, and often is. Les's and Lynn's therapies were trying and scary, but also enjoyable. Something was happening.

The therapist is upheld by therapy as well as upholds it. There is a kind of generic or primordial other that supports the entire situation. Both therapist and patient bathe or dip into it. Some call this other the therapeutic situation, the unconscious, parenting. There is no denying these factors. Yet I cannot help feeling there is something more. We are supported and torn apart by processes that give rise to ourselves, to therapy, parenting, intimations of unconscious functions, the great other that life is.

We cannot exhaust this great other by speaking about it. Our studies do not exhaust it. It continues, on and on. Some analysts, like artists, depict it in terms of atmospheric conditions, tonalities. Balint (1968) writes of an interpenetrating, harmonious mix-up of self and other, as if something like water or air were the medium through which self-other arise, blend, evolve. Freud used electrical as well as liquid images for psychic fluidity and intensity. Jung used alchemical and chemical images for transformation processes.

It can be argued that the poetic element in psychoanalysis is very strong. In some measure, psychoanalysis derives its power from the aliveness of its images, metaphors, and symbols. It makes real relationships (parents-children, therapist-patient) the stuff of poetry, and vice versa. It brings together actual relationships and imagination in ways that draw on scientific, religious, and artistic processes. What a web of actual and imaginative elements the therapeutic relationship is! No wonder one can develop a taste for it, or be put off!

Self gives rise to other, other to self. There is deep permeability in us, in all things. We grow by means of our permeability, without which there would be no learning. A universe without permeable beings, without learning, is unimaginable.

We are used to emphasizing the difference between subject and object in learning processes. We are different than the things we learn. Yet one of our secrets is that we learn by identifying with what we are learning about, by taking it into ourselves and entering into it. For some reason, we have become ashamed of the capacity to learn by uniting ourselves with the objects of our study. We have become ashamed of deep and passionate immersion.

We grow by identifying with various aspects of our selves and others. Some identifications are longer lasting than others. This gives rise to the fear that we will lose our selves forever in these identifications. We will not be ourselves but our identifications.

Therapy helps make us less fearful of identifications as we experience the kernel of self-identity that runs through our identifications. We come through myriad me/not-me elements and resurface through multitudes of identifications. To combine thoughts from Zen Buddhism and Judaism, our original face or naked being is rich in heritage. It would be awful to compromise either our nakedness or the associative streams of lifetimes.

How stilted and stultified one becomes if one always fights identifications. How jellyfish-like always to surrender to them. Surrender, like fighting, is necessary but provisional. There is more experiencing and learning on the other side of every identification. Identity and identification go on and on. There is always an open-ended element to what self and other might be.

Chapter Five

Mind-Body

In previous books and papers (1986, 1992, 1993), I have written about the importance of the mental-self/physical-self distinction in clinical work. The Cartesian distinction between mind-body is one version of a dualism that runs through cultures in many times and places. It is as if emphasis on different capacities takes us into different worlds of experience.

We can get into or out of our bodies with a shift of attitude. We can relish surface sensations or dip into deep, interoceptive, quasi-sensory streams. Sitting still, or moving in various ways, alters our sense of aliveness. Music and painting take us to different places, perhaps branches emanating from a common source. Sight, sound, and skin interweave beautifully. But they can make different claims, pull in different directions, and at times tear us apart.

There is belief in spirits of ancestors, the Great Spirit, the Spirit of Spirits, a soul that antedates and survives death, eternal mind. These are not just beliefs but experiences. One undergoes an experience that can be described as an eternal moment. It *feels* that way. The moment fades. The everyday self makes its claims. Yet the eternal moment echoes. We sense its waves. It uplifts us in the background of our beings. It bursts into the foreground again and again.

We can process our sense of infinitude-finitude in myriad ways, emphasizing contrast or interweaving. Different states, functions, and capacities feed and fight one another, depending on social-cultural and physical conditions, shifts of attitude and mood, and intangible mixtures of chance and disposition. The Bible is filled with human encounters with God. I have no doubt that many of these narratives express real experiences. Authentic experiential kernels or nuclear moments undergo alternate sets of elaborations. I do not doubt the authentic moments that yield the extravagance of Shiva or Kali or Vishnu or Brahma.

If religious experience is hallucination, so is much sexual experience. Cupid shoots arrows and we go mad, swept away by Eros. When we come down we may wonder, "What was *that* about?" Terrific, yes—beautiful, a great experience. We are lucky if it was just a happy interlude or if it turns into a decent relationship and the hard work begins. Literature is filled with tales of destruction following erotic delirium. The only difference between a sexual and religious hallucination may involve location and type of orgasm, and these distinctions get pretty blurry.

Common sense has no monopoly on sanity. What seems like common sense to one group may appear insane to another. Groups and subgroups develop their own codes for maintaining well-being and may resort to violence to enforce coherence. It may take centuries for a delusion that grips a civilization to lose hold as new quasi-hallucinatory ideologies set in. The ocean of images never stops.

Different ways of being a body or a mind come and go. Generations have their fashions and styles of relating to capacities: mind over matter, matter over mind, brawn and brain. What a stunning parade the varieties of mental-physical creations are. Turn the kaleidoscope, get a new state of being, another mind-body mix, another slant on being body-mind-spirit, another turn of the feeling-thinking-envisioning self.

No wonder individuals feel torn apart by capacities that nourish them. Drink deeply from body, drink deeply from mind, drink deeply from spirit. Swings from one state to another can be bewildering. How do we negotiate changes of states? How do we move *between* positions?

Now body feels more real, now mind, now vision. To a certain extent, it is a relief to turn from one to another, to play one off against the other. Enough body, enough mind, enough vision. What a relief to turn the whole thing off, to let it all go, to be nothing. Then body-mind-spirit start up again.

At times certain ways of being mind-body-vision seem to suit us. The kaleidoscope shifts and new mixes feel right, some more so than others. Suddenly the sense comes, "Ah, this is *it*. This is really me." Or "This is what it's all about!" Days, months, years later one may discover that one has lived the wrong *it*.

The patients in this book, Les and Lynn, wrestled with mind-body mixes that felt both wrong and right.

They tried different mixes on for size. They began to see how they were tyrannized by "wrong" mixes, mixes that ripped them apart or bound them too tightly together. In time they also learned how states that feel right can be as tyrannical as states that feel wrong. They learned to adopt a provisional attitude to different mixes.

States come and go and contribute in varied ways to a sense of the fullness of life. With help, Lynn and Les stretched to make room for varieties of themselves and others. Movement between identities is as freeing, pleasurable, and significant as the identities themselves. In therapy, Lynn and Les got a chance to turn the mind-body kaleidoscope until they hit on mixes that enabled them to move on with their lives.

Les's Guide

The guide in Les's boat dream (described in Chapter Two, pp. 31–34), set the tone for therapy work to come. Psychoanalysts sometimes have envisioned "cure" as building the patient's "observing ego" in working alliance or identification with the analyst's "observing ego." No such detachment characterized the boat journey dream. The guiding function was wisdom in action, a symbol of the intelligence that pervades psychosomatic life. The guide helped Les find the way through movement, not observation. Seeing was part of a larger flow or directional movement. The guide helped provide a framework that enabled psychic functions to work together.

Sea and snakes threatened to flood and poison the journey. They embodied split-off aspects of personality that Les could not wish away. The dream knit them into an overall movement. Water supported as well as menaced the boat. Snakes added cunning and energy, the same cunning and energy that Les spent fearing and fighting them.

Les intermittently followed the guide's messages. He began a business with his brother against his mother's wishes. He married and raised a family. He sought therapeutic help. But at critical moments he faltered and gave up. He abandoned his business like a sinking ship and poisoned his marriage. His link with the guiding aspect of the self broke down at critical points and gave way to paralysis, panic, and self-attack.

In the dream, the guide worked on the boat—the body. There was a connection between mental and physical aspects of self: each was part of the other and called the other into being. The guide cut through psychic divisions and permitted longed-for movement. In time, Les would be more able to follow the inner guide and realign himself with a destiny that he could say yes to. In time, he might recognize the guide as the voice of experience, his own voice of destiny. Before this could happen, Les would have to glimpse fault lines and splits in his personality, and wrestle with what went wrong.

Splitting and Spinning

Les spoke of what it was like to fall apart. He tried to handle his fear of flying by distancing himself from it.

He took off from his body to watch the trip from high above. He tried to contract himself into an observing ego far away from danger, flying above his body like the plane above the earth.

With mental ego in flight, body ego became hysterical. Les feared he would lose control and splatter in the aisle, a writhing heap of anxiety. Mental detachment and body chaos reinforced each other. Les kept the plane up by obsessive watching and thinking, while battling the urge to be incontinent.

The split turned into a spin. Tension between watching and the urge to splatter mounted. Les was torn apart by psychic systems flying in opposite directions. He started to whirl and drink himself into oblivion.

With therapeutic help, Les *saw* his mind going one way, his body another, and *experienced* the tension of his predicament in a premonitory way. Therapy acted as a filter through which he could experience his makeup in abbreviated fashion, rather than going through a raw, explosive impact each time. He became more used to himself and better able to encompass structures that tore him apart.

On the particularly important plane trip with his family, Les met his predicament by enjoying himself with other people, rather than watching-exploding and drinking himself into a stupor. He felt new. It was as if by locating the extremes of his nature, he moved beyond them. This happened spontaneously, after much hard work. He was still vulnerable. Nothing was "solved." But for a long moment he stepped out of his problems, out of the structural shell that tortured him. In a miraculous moment of grace, he located himself beyond the reach of his problems.

Up-Down Movement

The great battle Les fought was not only with his mother but with a terrifying force that gripped his life. A climactic dream tried to encapsulate and identify this force by calling it Neville the Devil (Chapter Two, pp. 50–54).

The dream focuses on a mental ego problem; piercing eyes aim at the body-soul in an attempt to brutalize and subjugate it. An evil, hate-filled mind tries to capture everything that matters to Les. Neville is the guiding function gone wrong, an evil complement of the good guide.

Neville lives at the top of a tower; evil descends from a high place. The old idea that body is sin and head virtue is too simplistic. The head cannot be counted on to be a good ruler. The opposite is true of Neville—an evil head, the head gone wrong. He tyrannizes the treasures of life.

The attitude that colors head or body is more important than which is on top or bottom at this or that moment. Insofar as Les's love for wife and children was filtered through Neville, it became tainted and destructive. In his dream, Les saw Neville's home. With horror, he saw how Neville took over his life and sought to rule his being. Les mustered his resources to join the fight against the evil attitude.

The battle Les won in his dream has no end. Les's victory over the devil in his head marked a direction, a theme. Never before had the fight been so intense or so fruitful. The result was a greater freedom of up-down movement. Les could use his own mind more, think his own thoughts, make a decision, allow a decision to grow. Dealing with Neville the Devil paved the way for Les to begin doing what he had to do to feel real and decent. Les's climactic battle precipitated his decision to move and start his own business. If Les had not stood up to the evil force (with help), I believe he would have remained mired indefinitely in his stagnant, angry life. Without facing the devil in his head, he would have remained his mother's slave.

Lynn's Confrontations with Mind-Body

Lynn dreamed of a fire in the basement that threatened top floors (Chapter Three, pp. 63–66). The fire below was associated with sex and rage. Lynn tried to stay on top of it, just as with sex she modulated excitement by being on top. She shut herself off if she were below, not in control. Lynn was caught in a war between her controlling mental ego (top) and pulsating body ego (below).

She paid for her controlling attitude with bouts of confusion and, finally, deadness. A too-controlling attitude might kill the fire. The dilemma for Lynn: Which was worse, the fire or its death? I believe Lynn's coming to therapy meant she was sensitive to the confusion and deadness that went along with her mental ego's superficial victory over life.

Lynn's inability to tolerate her fire worked against her creativeness and larger sense of self. When she came close to something inside herself, she turned off. If experience became too intense, she became confused and tended to douse it. The controls she hoped would see her through did not do justice to the depths of her being.

Thus, the tendency to shut out bodily states went far beyond modulations of sex and anger. At times she felt congealed into a knot behind her eyes—a compressed, dense core of controlling mind. This tense mental state actually could result in burning headaches, which diminished as therapy continued. Such concentrated effort at mental control was associated with a tightening of muscles throughout her body, including shoulders, lower back, and sphincters, which accounted for many of the bodily pains she complained about. It was as if a small, fearful, willful, angry mental ego commandeered her musculature to join in the defense efforts, a kind of mental-muscular armor (Reich, 1949; Federn, 1957; Elkin, 1972).

Lynn's mind-body tightness diminished a fuller sensory flow linked with intuition and a more nuanced, flexible array of feelings. It was very much to Lynn's credit that not only did she feel something was missing but that, in a poignant sense, she missed her self. She had intimations of a sensory, intuitive-feeling life that her mind-body knot shut out.

Blankness: The Mixmaster Function of Tension

A brittleness ran through Lynn's nature and warred with responsiveness. Tensions mounted and life came to a standstill. Lynn collapsed into blankness, a nameless tension. The blankness that she discovered was freeing, if disturbing.

Lynn experienced different kinds of blankness. Sometimes blankness was an irritable stupor leading nowhere, a tension that fed on itself, a numb paralysis. At other times, she experienced peacefulness scarcely known before. More often, blank tension bothered her; but the more she stood it, the more she grew.

In moments of blank tension, Lynn did not play opposites against each other. Did opposites dissolve, become irrelevant, find places in a larger whole, or did they stop being the focus of attention for a while? For a time, the mental ego contraction that trapped Lynn gave way. Mind-body boundaries became fluid. Areas of self that were usually kept apart whirled around together in indistinguishable ways—a blank, blinding whirl. Lynn sometimes spoke of blank tension as a mixmaster. It was less important to choose between top-bottom (mind-body) or hot-cold than the brews of experience they formed. The mixmaster function of tension itself became the medium through which opposites mixed, a blast of light containing all colors.

Contraction-Expansion: Return to Three-Dimensionality

The swirl and blur of anonymous tension involved a contraction of personality, a denudation of experience into a kind of flattened, electrical density. When the tension receded, Lynn returned to three-dimensional emotional life with a new appreciation for the everyday self. Mind-body distinctions reformed, but with a better working relationship, more open interweavings, and less fear and bitterness about what each contributed.

The naked blankness acted as a base from which states of everyday self rose and fell. Whether Lynn felt bigger or smaller, higher or lower, more in head or in body, blank intensity was a horizon that encompassed all these states, much like a black hole in space. The blank intensity was not pointless. Rather, the shifting stream of feelings contained in the intense blankness contributed to building personality.

For example, Lynn's rage had been vacuous and unfocused, with as little permanent effect as changing weather. Her rages grew out of wounded sensitivity, meaningful to her but to others more like angry outbursts than communications compelling serious attention. Her rage oscillated between the extremes of being trapped behind her eyes (mental ego) to pouring promiscuously and bitingly through her mouth like vomit or waste (body ego). Her anger sounded brittle, shrill, formless. Mind-body elements were not sufficiently coordinated to back each other up and have telling, fruitful impacts. There was not enough resonance behind her rage.

When Lynn blew up out of heightened blankness, her husband paid attention to her. He heard *her* through it. Seeing and feeling came together in the blankness. *She* was in her body; *she* was in her mind. *She* was not limited by either. *She* came through her outburst. Her rage rose up from nowhere to her belly, through her heart, and coupled with seeing. Her rage now had backbone, and its truth helped clear the air.

Heightened blankness and three-dimensional living are centers/horizons for each other. Lynn became aware of the movement between blankness and vibrant multiplicity, and of her need for both. She moved between the white blast of tension that dissolved and reshuffled differences and the head-mind/body-mind interweaving that provided structure for growth and use of thoughts and feelings. Instead of being the victim of whims and uncontrollable surges that battled brittleness, she held fast to a mysterious partnership with oscillating planes of existence. A nulling tension made her feel more fulfilled, more able to spread into life. She lived more fully in this movement than in the clash of wills. Her emotional life took on added authority and vulnerability.

Mind-Body Capacities Enable Self-Other

It is odd that the same capacities that give us ourselves make us seem strange to ourselves. The fact that we have such a wide range of physical and mental possibilities contributes to this strangeness.

What fantastic beings we are! We bathe in seas of sensations: warm sun, cool breeze, encompassing water, brown-green earth with blue-white above, slow arousals that go on for days, orgasmic showers, bliss of movement, thin surfaces of pleasure beneath the skin, the "no" of too much, a heart that says "I love you" in the night when no one is there, tenderness, rage when things go wrong, fear that they might not right themselves, body-to-body bliss, feeling-to-feeling joy, mind-to-mind ecstasy.

Thoughts tick. Everything is monitored, evaluated, criticized. Passion breeds obsession. There is a need to see things as they are, to break illusion, to undo eros and longing, to go the other way.

Images flow. Sensation, feeling, thinking feed one another. Physical and mental mirror each other. Images make comparisons from one realm to another. Snakes of meaning weave through all levels of being, gathering them, spilling meaning (poison or nectar) everywhere. Life is poetry.

Life is also action. We survive, make a living. Practical tasks save us from nonsense, threaten to kill the spirit, bury us with fatigue. Immersion in everyday life makes us real, worth something. Some persons triumph, go to the top, become rich, famous, powerful. Some make discoveries, produce inventions. We learn how to do things. We do the best we can. We come and go. There is a vast bottom: casualties, bombs may strike anywhere. There is also a vast, bottomless support system, as shaky as the earth.

What kinds of beings are we? Some of us believe in soul, even in soul travel. Spirit leaves body, goes here and there, returns. We *feel* this. We elaborate systems of separation and return, from revenge to ethics of purification—transcendence of spirit, transmutation of body, salvation. Others among us say there is no soul, no spirit, no choice. We pull back, contract boundaries, study ourselves, then dance and play. We are and are not our intellect, intelligence, willpower. At times all that matters is flow of feeling, feeling free. We may feel imprisoned by either physical or mental self. The physical self may be too fusional, too explosive, and the mental self may be overcontrolling. We may feel imprisoned by both our physical and mental selves and try to blow them away. At other times, our physical and mental selves may make us feel freer. Our thoughts and feelings become both friends and enemies. We are gods who do not want to be contained by images and destroy pictures we make of ourselves. Pictures are prisons. We feel restricted by our capacities and live like boomerangs.

What a relief it is to contract into a particular identity, although, in time, our identities begin to squeeze the air out of us.[1] We are wounded by our identities. We wound ourselves with them. We make injurious judgments about who we are or aren't, rubbing our noses in fatal flaws, torturing ourselves with the feeling that something is wrong, or at least never right enough. "It's not fair," we hear children say. It's not fair to be saddled with this identity, this awful problem.

Body and mind simply cannot solve mental and physical problems. Or, rather, they do so only in limited ways. We make inroads and this affords much pleasure, but fatal flaws remain. We never stop rubbing ourselves and one another the wrong way. If we are lucky, we do not merely irritate the same old wound for nought. The wound deepens, and we deepen with it.

---

[1]See Corrigan and Gordon (1995) for their account of how mind-body splits can lead to contracted identity formations.

Our mental and physical capacities wound us, but we love using them. Maturation involves shifting the way we sound our wounds—a shift in resonance, a shift in the quality of coming through or growing around our wounds.

Les and Lynn were tied in knots by their physical and mental capacities. Lynn sank below them in emptiness, and Les pushed against them in struggle. Capacity below capacities, capacity against capacities. Each rubbed against or bounced off limitations of their own equipment without knowing it. It is through our equipment that we have access to our selves, our worlds, our faiths, our passions, our knowings. Yet we are acutely aware of how our point of access limits what we can be and know. We stare at limits of our field of being and try to enlarge the periphery. We jump into and slide through funnels.

Les and Lynn were oppressed by their selves without knowing it. There are enough outer oppressors to keep one busy for a lifetime. People benefit from therapy by talking about their oppressors. One needs to rage about one's wounds, mourn losses (including loss of what one never had). To stop oppression, one may need to play a role in history. The struggle to right wrongs is noble and necessary. However, in therapy one can let down and see that both therapist and patient are oppressed by who they are. One gets past therapist as oppressor. In essence, what makes one paranoid, depressed, or joyous is the incessant ticking of basic capacities. Mind-body capacities and self-other dramas keep pulsating and structuring one another. Oppressive attitudes in self and society restructure one another.

It is not enough to talk about self-other dramas that make up one's life. One must also probe mind-body capacities that make self-other dramas possible. One must get a sense of what kinds of drama our equipment can constitute and how this equipment works in our particular life. Our special torturers mediate the torturing capacity in general, and one must come to grips with both particular and generic aspects of this capacity.

It is good for therapy to become the torturer for a time. Therapy is like a magnet drawing out torturers in an individual's personality. The therapist as torturer becomes a stand-in for torture as such. With careful work, one discriminates nuances of the torturing processes and the spectrum of torturers: parents, siblings, self, society, and a variety of other devils. Favorite forms of torture receive the most attention.

Torture never stops, but room is made for it. A person discovers he is more than the sum of his torturers. The holy spark is not annihilated by all one's demons. One survives the holy spark as well. Polarities are parts of broader, continuing processes. The good feeling that comes from working long and hard with personal traps is worth honoring. It is not simply that we are bought off by good feeling, or that we work in order to feel good; it is a real grace that good feeling comes through hard work on ourselves.

So many ways of exercising mind or body make us feel good or bad. Freud points out that we have a free-floating capacity for pleasure and pain that can take many forms. Part of our plasticity as a species involves the many ways we produce pleasure—although, once organized, group and individual styles of seeking pleasure tend to be persistent.

Violence and good feelings often go together, as in childbirth, as in destroying infidels or rivals, as in kidding oneself. Yet good feelings can also go together with being a better person, and this is a treasure. Lynn and Les felt better because of therapy *and* became better persons. Ways that mind and body bothered them led to using mind and body better. Fears that therapy makes one more selfish and self-absorbed are very understandable. But therapy can also make one a better neighbor, parent, mate, child, worker, and a more caring, productive person. There *can* be ethics in good feelings.

Levinas (1969, p. 78 and Section 3, Part B) writes that "ethics is the spiritual optics." The sense of goodness a baby gets by staring at its mother's face is the basis of morality. Morality is not merely something imposed upon experience; it flows from deep within it. I believe this goodness is the core and context for what happens in therapy. All excesses or deficits necessary to any moment are united by a goodness that runs through them. We try to outlast and outflank what is horrible, to give basic goodness a chance.

Therapy organizes itself around the face of the therapist. The face of the therapist encompasses many aspects. It contains openness, caring, receptivity. It contains dead spots, fear, anger, emptiness. If one reads soul in eyes, the therapist's soul is an open book, like the patient's. The therapist's face is ordinary, special, bright, stupid, circumspect, diligent. Sometimes it is alive or filled with well-being, sometimes tired or hungry. It is everything a person is. But the therapist is there to help, at whatever level of being, ability, competence, or grace is available. In every session, faith is lived and tested, faith that the human self can come through itself and others, that good will out. There is an invisible, radiant heart in the face of the therapist, informed and inspired, speaking to the true face shining in all hearts.

I don't think Lynn or Les needed to test basic goodness to the utmost. Some people break it down until there seems to be nothing left. Some people so dismantle themselves and others, or are so dismantled by life, that it seems cruel to speak of faith in the goodness of goodness. Lynn and Les did not go that far. They broke their personalities down only far enough to make realignment possible. Lynn and Les never lost faith in life, not in an ultimate way.

Their respective therapies took place in a context of faith. To be sure, they tested this faith. Much in their personalities bent towards mistrust. They spent a lot of time expecting to be wronged, ready to fight. It was easy to find fault with therapy and to be mistrustful; I gave plenty of room for mistrust and fighting. But therapy did not get killed off. Love kept resurfacing through mistrust and fear until Lynn and Les went through what they had to in order to discover and create the experiences they needed to move on.

In retrospect, I think that Lynn was bored with herself. I believe this was something I felt when I first saw her but could not put into words until later. She did not act bored. But, in fact, she was going around in circles. She basically had the same old thoughts, fell into the same old ways; she fought the same battles with the same mental/physical tools. I think she was bored by her own capacities. She had gotten to the end of what she could do with the level of life she had achieved.

Lynn hid her boredom by being enthralled with her own personality and her will to triumph in the domain she had carved out for herself. She glistened with herself, put the best face on, tried to keep a bit above herself and her life. Her husband did this, too. They were too busy to be bored.

But almost as soon as she had a chance her usual ways of using mind and body fell away, as though she could not wait to get rid of them. She fell to a place beneath them, a place that they could not spoil. She went to a place that did not bore her—her emptiness—where usual ways of using mind and body were helpless. Now she would have to discover something new. Empty tension filled her. It was scary and wounding and wondrous, a torture that got her somewhere. Lynn's emptiness put her usual mind-body set on hold in a sort of creative paralysis.

On the other hand, therapy provided a context that enabled Les to experience his mind and body breaking apart and spinning around each other. His emphasis was on movement—manic, desperate movement. Like Lynn, his ideology of control broke down. Unlike Lynn, he did not simply drop to another place. Rather, his control systems parodied themselves by going into superspin. His mistrustfulness was not wrong, but it needed to find the right targets.

The otherness of the therapy horizon is big and wise enough to let use of mind-body capacities snap into place. Therapist and patient alike dip into and benefit from the otherness of therapy processes. Both are supported, corrected, and inspired by an intimate otherness that can redirect the ways in which we use our mind-body capacities and make a significant difference in our lives.

Chapter Six

Faith and Catastrophe

Disaster or catastrophe must be recognized as a fundamental category of human existence. Death and debility can strike at any time. Things do not go as we want. We worry about survival. We worry about how well we will survive.

The sense of disaster permeates our beings. It runs through our bodies. It is part of the atmosphere we breathe. We are told not to be afraid, but fear is part of our equipment. We are taught from early on to lie about fear, to make believe we are not afraid, to act as if everything is normal. It *is* normal to feel danger as part of situations. Fear and danger can heighten sensitivity to moment-to-moment living and make us feel more alive.

Too often Freud is caricatured as imagining people ought to be untroubled pleasure-seekers. Nothing could be further from the truth. The world he portrayed was riddled with pain and sorrow, anxieties and wounds. If libido was a great river of pleasure, it met with endless obstacles. If sensitivity yielded to bliss, it was also subject to terror, injury, and rage.

Freud's depictions of people in distress were beyond the pleasure principle from the outset. For Freud, the primal trauma was "flooding" (1895; Masson, 1985). Our psychophysical equipment can produce stimulation that it cannot handle. Even a nerve needs recovery time after firing. In more dramatic fashion, the psyche shuts down in the face of its own intensity. The flow of libido can be wounded by external events, but personality can also be wounded by its own energy as affective storms break down functioning. Freud's writings on the death drive, whatever their merit, heightened awareness of areas of psychic deadness and led to many descriptions of self-deadening and numbing processes.

Winnicott (1974) linked fear of breakdown with breakdowns that already had taken place in infancy, when equipment was too undeveloped to handle demands on it. Bion (1970) wondered whether the birth of psychic life was a catastrophe or had catastrophic elements—a kind of psychic big bang, a suffering into being. He depicted numerous ways in which individuals avoided, killed, or emptied their own aliveness. One gets a sense from these writers that there are conditions in which the psyche may be too much for itself, that sensitivity is more than we can bear, that life collapses under its own weight, and that the tendency to denude ourselves of experience and die-out is widespread.

In all individuals there are areas of partial collapse, deficit, and lack of development. Our attitude to these areas is crucial. We deform ourselves not only by secret weakness and madness but by our attitude to weakness and madness. Despair is realistic. It is based on undeniable awareness of limitations.

Religious faith explodes or dissolves limitations. The lame walk, the blind see, the weak are strengthened, the ill are healed, the twisted are made straight, the dead return to life. Faith tells us not to despair. Faith moves mountains and parts seas of personality, so that we are no longer obstacles to ourselves. We are no longer our own hell but find heaven within.

Despair and faith, the great twins forever wrestling. If one looks closely, the picture blurs. There are many kinds of faith and despair, many gradations, levels, qualities. Great wars in history are not between faith and despair but between alternate faiths.

Despair can be unrealistic if it goes too far. People are crushed by depression, sealed off in despair. On the other hand, battlefields of faith are filled with sacrifices to manias. We are blessed with lows and highs of experience. Both are part of the color of life and contribute to creative processes. The movement between depressive and ecstatic affect is part of what makes life worth living, but it can cause great havoc.

It is with relief that we turn to our capacity for rational problem-solving. We study requirements of situations and see what processes are made of. We use cognitive abilities to get a balancing take on things. We do not have to be victimized by moods and circumstances but learn to work with limitations and positive aspects of capacities. We learn to use multiple capacities to modulate one another.

Still, a voice nags, "Is this all there is?" Are our ecstatic-depressive seizures primitive or pathological? Are our crazy affective depths for nought? What is the best in us? What kind of beings are we?

Cheer and gloom combine and separate in myriad ways. Their movement is part of the color of life, of self. Cheer and gloom fight and feed each other. At times both pop into the emotional blender and mix so thoroughly that the result is a wonderfully peaceful mood. Too often they tyrannize each other. Most often, cheer and gloom go their separate ways, with no point in common, no fruitful tension to ensure progress to psychological wholeness.

People are usually more prone to one mood than another. Certain emotions and sets of emotions are apt to dominate a life. One's sense of identity tends to take a certain emotional atmosphere as home base; other emotions are considered necessary, nourishing, and interesting, but somewhat alien. We can traverse ranges of emotions and feel differently for a time, but most often we bob up in seas of shifting feelings with our dominant emotions around us like a tire.

It takes a certain faith to affirm or make peace with one's dominant emotion while staying open to changing states and the impact of other emotional atmospheres. It is tragic if one rejects one's dominant feelings because they are not what one would like them to be. It is equally destructive if one is so attached to this dominant state that other emotions are not only strangers but enemies.

Throughout the ages, the deep faith required to encourage a generous-spirited openness that allows our selves to expand and grow with the other has battled with a one-sided view that fosters a distrustful rejection of the unfamiliar. An expansive faith works to welcome the other and incorporate its positive aspects within the self. So many stories tell us how the welcomed stranger or guest transforms our lives, while the rejected one ushers in tragedy.

Yet life events also teach us the value of contraction for survival. At times expansiveness can destroy us. We shrink from all but the accustomed, and there seems to be no way out of these swirling Möbius strips. What we are in need of is a faith big and open enough to embrace all contradictions of living, a faith that incorporates practicality with a radiant grace that allows our selves to expand in new and unexpected directions.

Psychotherapy is one of the battlegrounds on which individuals struggle to reach a larger faith. People try to squeeze themselves into lives that pinch and distort them. Indeed, they feel pinched and distorted by their very selves. Their personalities do not fit a deeper sense of what they feel they are or might be. In psychotherapy we learn to welcome the stranger that is ourselves.

We become a bit more hospitable to the contradictions and vagaries of real living. What is strange and familiar shifts. The strange becomes familiar and the familiar strange. We are carried along not only by the stream of events but by a breathtaking interweaving and inner unfolding of these events. We learn to appreciate the texture and background atmosphere of our lives, not only its heroic moments. We grow through shifting combinations of sacrifice, surrender, and assertion. There are choices and directions we struggle with and fight for. But there is also openness, permeability, interweaving.

People like Lynn and Les seek the help of psycho-therapy because of an impending sense of catastrophe or because of a catastrophe that has already hit. Some-times the catastrophe is silent. It may take years for someone to realize that he or she has lived the wrong life or no life. People chronically over- and underesti-mate what they are up against. Only as time goes on does one begin to sense consequences of a direction taken long ago.

It took Lynn and Les years to connect with the sense that something catastrophic had happened to their lives, and to them. A sense of catastrophe was part of the background of existence for each of them, yet they were strong enough to ignore it and go about the business of living. A sense of aliveness filled their sails and propelled them past catastrophic anxieties. There were enough good things in living to hold their attention and struc-ture their activities. Nevertheless, it did not take much for life to punch holes in their self-regard, so that their well-being wavered as variable doses of catastrophic dread broke though.

For years Lynn and Less managed their underlying catastrophic anxieties one way or another. They told themselves, "It's not the end of the world." Or "It won't kill you. You're not going to die. It's not so bad. It could've been worse." Or "Keep it in perspective. Don't run away with yourself. Don't go off the deep end." There are any number of phrases that all of us use in an attempt to stop anxiety from spiralling.

154

Faith and Catastrophe

Like most of us, Lynn and Les expected to be derailed from time to time. Our sense of continuity includes momentary and even longer breakdowns. We tell ourselves that this is part of living, the ups and downs, twists and turns to be expected along the rocky road of life. Songs tell us that every cloud has a silver lining, that we can pick ourselves up after we fall, that goodness triumphs over injury.

But there come times when catastrophe management techniques break down and do not reconstitute well enough. If efforts of people close to us are useless, or part of the problem, we may reach out for professional help. We hope the other can supply the processing ability we lack and jumpstart or offset deficits in our selves.

In a way, Lynn came to therapy for help in breaking down. Without quite realizing it, she felt imprisoned by her angry, controlling mind, a sliver of herself. She sought therapy to expand, to thaw out, to become more herself. This required going through moments of enormous disorganization as she strove to drop the constant guard she kept. In therapy, Lynn could let go and experience ordinary good feelings and court a range of untasted states. Little by little, she was better able to encompass agonies around which she had constricted. Her faith in life deepened as she opened herself up in the face of her fears.

Les, in contrast, located the origins of his sense of catastrophe with his mother. She impacted on him like an atom bomb, yet was a source of support and nourishment. He was terrified that if he grappled with her catastrophic impact he would lose her as a source of nourishment, even though he no longer needed or wanted this nourishment. He pushed past his catastrophic anxieties until he could bear them no longer. For Les, the sense of catastrophe became all-consuming, in spite of his attempts to limit it to his fear of flying. By the time he sought help, he felt on the verge of going over the brink. Les never quite lost faith in life, but his faith was sorely challenged.

In therapy, bits of faith nibble on bits of disaster. Whether one locates the source of disaster in oneself, in others, or in uncontrollable events, faith has its job cut out. Faith metabolizes disaster, and disaster makes faith realistic. Discontent eggs the personality on. As Lynn and Les discovered, the parts of an individual do not fit together easily. The lack of fit, the misfit, may be catastrophic, but it also can force an individual's best efforts and lead to unanticipated psychic territory. The attempt to reshape oneself and one's life is endless.

Les's Sense of Disaster

In therapy Les found himself at the heroic center of a nightmarish world. Horrible fears and agonies oppressed him. In his inner life, with which his mother could not help him, one danger after another appeared.

Les was torn between therapy and his mother, only to realize that this conflict masked the struggle between the wish to grow and to maintain the status quo. Standing up to himself and his mother went together. He located the best and worst moments of his life, the moments in which he was most truly himself in bliss and agony. His heart told him he would have to take his family and start his own business, which meant starting life on another plane.

Les tried to organize his sense of catastrophe around a specific fear-of-flying phobia, but this fear was a concentrated pocket of more generalized terror. He had repeated nightmares about his children's and his own kidnapping and murder. He panicked at the idea of breaking his mother's domination and going his own way. The terror that gripped him in the air mimicked an inner disaster that marred his sense of self. Dread of catastrophe permeated his life.

Disaster and the Sense of Triumph

In his best dreams Les triumphed over dangers. The grandiose self won. The narcissism his mother nurtured turned against her. She catered to Les's narcissism only if he obeyed her. Nevertheless, he derived strength from her fusional control. Their closeness made him feel valuable as well as worthless. Deep inside he felt there was something worth fighting for.

Even with all his problems, Les functioned well in social, vocational, and family life. He managed to control or play down pockets of madness. The gratification he got out of his sense of triumph and control enabled him to postpone getting help for years. An underlying sense of disaster and hopelessness made him cling to areas of triumph and control more tenaciously.

157

It was natural for Les to try to control therapy. Like a good businessman, Les tried to be on top, to treat therapy like a deal. He used a therapy language culled from pop literature and the press. He framed therapy as a battle between the "neurotic self" and "healthy self" (his words). My job was to help him strengthen the latter. Neurotic meant fearful and destructive; healthy meant loving and capable. Much therapy experience was captured by this net of words. Nevertheless, the fact that Les spoke about his catastrophic foreboding over an extended period of time had an effect that simplistic language could not dispel. Although Les defined his struggle, his struggle also found ways to define and touch him.

Disaster and Horror: Splitting and Spinning

Therapy encouraged the splits that marked Les's personality to stand out. The magnetic function of therapy caused everything wrong with him to come to the fore, all the bad stuff to pour out. Les's mind-body splits were especially magnified on plane trips. Leaving the ground provided an image and stimulus for mental-self/body-self and self-mother separation and loss of support. In the air, stakes were high and natural fears skyrocketed. Once off the ground it was as if mind and body and self and other would never get together again. Les would spin out of existence or crash.

Before therapy, Les drank himself into oblivion. Through therapy, splitting and spinning and crashing found voices. Les had never spoken from these places before, not fully. There had been no way for him to explore these horrors. He lacked the tools and setting. He did not know it was possible to delineate internal divisions carefully, respectfully, feelingly, dramatically. That he was more than the sum of his divisions and terrors was a stunning discovery—an immediate, deeply felt experience.

Les's splitting-spinning is described in detail in Chapters Two and Five. What needs to be emphasized at this juncture is the sense of disaster that permeates splitting-spinning. There are alternative ways to conceptualize the relationship between splitting-spinning and the sense of disaster. Splitting may be a defensive way of dealing (or not dealing) with painful states and conflicts. Splitting-spinning also can result from prolonged unbearable pain and insoluble conflicts. In the former case, splitting helps to organize the personality's response to difficulty. In the latter, splitting is part of the personality's spin into oblivion in the face of unendurable failure. Defensive splitting-spinning can harden into rigid personality structure, while splitting-spinning in response to intense pain and conflict is part of an emptying out of personality owing to failure of equipment.

The two movements (defense against pain, collapse owing to pain) are subsystems of the same personality, working with and against each other in complex ways. Splitting contributes to obsessive and paranoid organizations that feed on areas of partial collapse. Obsessive-paranoid, rigid mental-self structures thrive on areas of body-self formlessness. Hyper mental control and mindless explosiveness alternate.

Les's life was an endless circle of fighting and fucking. His strengths and weaknesses so intertwined that they confused him. Paranoid explosiveness linked with loss mushroomed in dreams that threatened to obliterate psychic structure entirely; nightmares blow themselves up with their own terror. Plane trips heightened personality dissociations that Les tried to solve by intensifying mental-self structures. In these states, oblivion was achieved not only by body-self fusion-explosiveness (loss of control) but also by mental-self hyperspin (mental-self whirling out of existence by its own hyperactivity).

I have repeatedly mentioned that much in Les's life was good. Les made good business deals, had good sex, participated in good moments with his children. He enjoyed the exercise of his powers and his triumphs over fears. But his terrors were never far away. They might rise up at any moment to haunt or obliterate him. So much of his life was spent over a hole that could open at any time. He sensed that his own solutions made matters worse, that his equipment was stained with terror. He could no more escape horror than he could jettison his psychophysical equipment. He helplessly willed himself through life, while his equipment oscillated among pleasure, torment, and hellish spins to nowhere.

Faith, Nightmare, and Pockets of Goodness

To the extent that he was able, Les underwent the agony of experiencing how torn apart he was. He came to therapy to let what was broken and missing have a say.

A link was established between nightmares and helpless rage and panic. Nightmarish aspects of childhood returned. They formed the background of his life. It dawned on him how like a nightmare his waking life had been. Not only was he afraid of mother's disappearance, but for the first time he could say that *he* was afraid of disappearing. What a struggle it was to stay visible and have a say, to be a person among persons, a machine among machines.

Les came through dangers in his dreams, which were never far from nightmares, with the help of male figures. The background father came to the foreground. My orientation and being, together with the therapy atmosphere and task, stimulated the somnolent father and released Les's own inner guide. It also released the enemy.

The image of Neville the Devil organized everything that Les most feared. Neville was a caricature of warped power, greed and ambition, the will to be on top, the bringer of loss. He would take everything, leaving Les nothing. The miracle was that Les stood up to him.

The battle between healthy and neurotic sides achieved more dignity by being linked with the struggle between good and evil. Les stood up to the evil self. He battled his own twistedness. Neville was not merely neurotic; he was evil. "Evil" was in his name. Les needed to reach beyond parlor psychology to make contact with his plight. His personal catastrophe was also a moral catastrophe. The history of his prior inability to withstand the Neville force went hand in hand with loss of integrity and a muted conviction that his life was a lie.

Les did not like living a lie but felt helpless to extricate himself. Therapy fanned his longing to set things right. Therapeutic goodness is more precise than ordinary good feelings. It locates and studies psychic barriers, blocks, deficits, conflicts, parasitic attitudes, hidden sources of fear and inertia. Les's sexual, family, and business pleasures may have kept faith in life alive, but they did not help him get better. They did not change him. He clung to them for dear life and used them to compensate for the basic feeling that something was wrong. One tries to wash away nightmares with pleasures and cherish pockets of goodness, but the feeling that something is "off" continues.

It strengthened Les to realize that he was up against a devil. It is terrifying to see a devil but also a relief to have an image for madness, evil, sickness, weakness, and the horrifying aspect of being a human subject. Yes, something was wrong, very wrong, and the devil gave it habitation and a name. Les did not have to pretend *it* was not there.

Neville personified everything that intimidated Les and kept him down, including his own warp. Since childhood, Les had tried to push past fears but solved nothing. Les's personal fighting had been a diffuse, unfocused barrage, more a protest against impotence than a fight to the finish. Why did fighting work now?

Les made use of precision support to experience the thing that felt wrong, the "off" point or sick spot. Therapy gave Les practice in locating and working with sore spots and mobilized him to move toward the factor in his life that felt wrong. Therapy also excited Les's conviction that life was worth fighting for, to the point that he was willing to fight to the death. In a moment of total lucidity and obliviousness to self, Les let go and gave his all.

He exploded against the poison that was in him. Such an explosion into health is a moment of faith. One lets go of little pockets of goodness that keep one going and risks all for a deeper sense of good.

Faith and Repetition

Only when Les fought with all his might did he see what a fraud his devil was. For a moment he was free and fresh. Life teemed with possibilities. Yet Les could fight with all his might precisely because the devil cannot die like a real person. The devil is real but also a structure, a source, a principle or attitude, an eternal state. The free and fresh moment may be a joy forever, but it does not fill the psychic field long. The sick spot reforms and the fight continues.

Therapy gave Les a chance to rehearse catastrophic dreads and personality weaknesses thoroughly. He needed to go over and over his panicky outrage, seductive-controlling ploys, and dread of helplessness. He rehearsed the worst events in his life and enumerated the ways he bent himself out of shape to handle them. He let the shock, disbelief, and horror that underscored his existence have room.

Repetition gives a person a chance to get used to himself. We repeat in order to learn. In therapy we become more familiar with the alphabet of psychic life in order to write a better story. Patients come to therapy because they are mired in stagnant or destructive repetition. Therapeutic repetition enables people to stretch into what they are stuck in. The stuck point, in turn, stimulates therapeutic activity and growth.

Furthermore, therapeutic repetition enables a person to move along his central lifeline. The knot of self coiled in stomach, backbone, and chest unwinds. The subject develops a taste for dropping below his "official personality" and moving into the thing that is wrong, working from square one. The perennial surprise is that by going deeper into one's "off" point, life moves more along its main axis.

The moment of faith is not the only moment, but it is a master moment. The sense of coming through what is wrong becomes a reference point, a foundation. One meets impasse points all through one's life and gains from doing so. When faith informs repetition, repetition becomes renewal.

Lynn: Good Feelings, Disturbances

Lynn felt good most of the time. I believe her good feelings came from being loved. Parents, siblings, friends, and husband loved her. Lynn appreciated herself. Yet she was not satisfied sailing through life on good feelings. Coming to therapy was a sign of dissatisfaction.

Disturbances spilled over in Lynn's dreams: the fire in the basement, the cracked freezer, the mouse that grew bigger and more uncontrollable. Good feelings do not wash away disturbances in dreams.

In fact, much in Lynn's life disturbed her: her father's inertia, her mother's invasiveness, her husband's self-absorption, injustice in the workplace, her brother's destructiveness. Lynn coated disturbances by being the helper. She tried to help deficient, weak, insensitive, ill, or angry others. Disturbances were foreign intrusions, out there in the other.

If bad feelings threatened to overwhelm good feelings, Lynn buttressed the latter by increasing her sense of rightness. She was the diagnostician *par excellence*. She saw what was wrong with the other, what needed correction. Her sense of being right picked up where pleasure left off. By filling herself with goodwill, she escaped finding sources of disturbance within herself.

In time, feeling and being good became disturbing, insofar as well-being stole her from herself. Feeling good became an index of muted dread. I think Lynn came to therapy to unwrap herself from the sticky goodness that coated her.

The Persona of Normalcy

Lynn found relief from dread of helplessness by nursing or lecturing others. She imagined benevolence as omnipotent. Lynn's helpfulness was part of her persona of normalcy. Her goodwill, diagnostic expertise, and energy *ought* to be enough to change others. It was difficult for Lynn to grasp that others remained the same despite her efforts. Her benevolence was not the key to other people's personalities.

Lynn sought help when she reached the brink of realizing that normalcy and goodness had failed her. The idea that goodness, especially her own goodness, was not enough to solve the problems of life shook her to the core. She could not deal with this realization alone. She feared she had nothing to fall back on.

Where goodness failed, rage threatened to break through. Efforts to reform others increased. She tried to bind fear and fury by increasing the dose of "rightness." If all she had to fall back on were rage, surely her life would be destroyed. Repentance was alien to her. She could not let down and simply own her fear and fury. She pinned her rage on the other's faults and obdurateness, the other's refusal to let her goodness be effective.

In her marriage, Lynn's goodness was incendiary. Her goodness stuck pins in her husband. Her role as the helpful and healthy one infuriated him. Her rightness added fuel to the fire. She possessed an explosive goodness. Her earnest and relentless accuracy threatened to blow her life sky high. She was on the verge of learning that no one could deal with her, and that she could not deal with herself.

The problem was complicated in that Lynn's "normalcy" and "goodness" contained much that really was normal and good. She could not have sustained her helping position for so long without real health to draw on. Change meant loss. Lynn felt she had too much to lose by changing. She feared her world would crumble if she were not the good and healthy one. Nevertheless, life forced her to look beyond her goodness. If her marriage were to succeed, she would have to move beyond "rightness."

Faith and Shock

In therapy Lynn collapsed to her weak point and saw how helplessness and benevolent impotence fed each other. Her glimpse of fear and helplessness shocked her. She was used to viewing herself as competent and scarcely believed so much unordered life swirled within her. Lynn courageously dipped in and out of her shock, touching it, withdrawing, embracing it, going into it a little more. A wordless sea of endless shock lay below her sense of control.

Her shock spread to many areas of her life. Seeing her mother with nephew Josh shocked Lynn into heightened awareness of the "good girl" induction she had been subjected to. It was shocking to see how much brainwashing goes on in childhood, such induction into slavishness. It was a relief to side with baby Josh's spontaneity and resistance. Lynn felt suffocated by her own goodness and the way it channeled spontaneity and natural assertiveness. Her own being made her claustrophobic. No wonder people try so hard to get away from themselves.

Lynn experienced the shock of recognition and horror at what had happened to her baby soul. She tasted the shock of being more like her mother than she could bear. It seemed that Lynn had been in an unconscious state of shock most of her life. An underlying shock kept her tied in knots, frozen, rigid. Once in therapy, Lynn followed a gradient that took her from shock to shock. During sessions she burrowed into the shock that silenced her. Her shock became a kind of cocoon in which she floated on currents of fear, streams of strange and unknown feelings, electrical stillness. She discovered many nuances of paralysis.

From still shock, rage pierced her confusion. To scream is an act of faith. Lynn's shock was a container for faith. She raged against the degradation that paralyzed her. She broke silence not by streams of words, but by a cry from gut and heart. This was not a cry of accusation and self-pity, not simply a hurt ego cry. The new cry broke through the frozenness. It was possible for words to matter more after such a scream.

Odd to say, but through paralysis Lynn became freer. Lynn's personality blanked out in shock and scream. Afterwards, her tears were warmer, part of thawing out. Most of her crying had been icy anger. Her shock was a kind of navel from which a deeper connection to herself grew.

The Uncontrollable Mouse

Today the unconscious is often represented by a mouse rather than a dragon (Eigen, 1986, pp. 322–327). This is, in part, an outgrowth of the need to wish the unconscious away. People want to reduce psychic life to the practical ego: Everything should be capable of practical management, goal-directed behavior, successful means-end relationships. The unconscious is made light of, joked about, treated like a mouse. The practical ego becomes complacent in its management of affects.

In Lynn's mouse dream (Chapter Three, pp. 90–94), Andy and Lynn tried to keep the mouse in its place and get rid of it by hitting it, Andy with his hand and Lynn with hand and book. The more they hit, the bigger the mouse grew. It bit Lynn's hand and would not let go. Neither physical power nor knowledge made it go away.

Lynn's psyche would not sit up and lick her hand like a pet. It refused to give in to superficial training, nor could it be eliminated by casual violence. The mouse would not conspire with an ethics of convenience. It was a nuisance, and it hurt.

Lynn spontaneously associated the mouse with baby activity, especially activity that scared her mother. Her mother could not handle the mouse that grew bigger and bit. Perhaps growth itself was biting. The growing baby did not fit parental/societal schemas and had to be filtered through various parental/societal limitations. Lynn had to live through parental fear of the baby self, a catastrophic underpinning to be renegotiated throughout her lifetime. Insofar as society tries to step on the baby mouse, it gets bigger and more vicious.

Through neglect and fear and beatings, Lynn's mouse threatened to become monstrous. If Andy and Lynn kept hitting it (with ego mastery ideology), it might grow so big as to leave no room to be hit, no room for Andy and Lynn at all. Lynn would have to develop some other way to relate to the mouse, the elusive demands of the baby self.

As Lynn became more able to enter into partnership with her psyche, her sense of herself became more problematic. Perception of difficulties proliferated. It was as if a global sense of catastrophe (fire) prismatically splintered into specific smaller disasters (mouse). Lynn was less overwhelmed by unconscious despair over her problems and more capable of facing herself a bit (mouse) at a time.

A first reflex to internal trouble is to shut it out or in some way get rid of it. One would like to wish trouble away. In the external world, we can kill a mouse and put out a fire. But we cannot get rid of our selves as long as we are alive. In our internal world, a fire can become a mouse for a time, but to count on long-term facile mastery can be disastrous. Lynn's challenge was to develop the capacity to let experience build. Like the mouse, something in her would not let go. She could not wish herself away, so she held on until she forced self-recognition. Like the mouse, Lynn was persistent and would not be pushed away, not by parents, bosses, husband, me, or, especially, herself.

Trauma After Trauma

Lynn felt good after working on the mouse dream, but it was not long before the next image of trauma appeared. Good work and good feelings do not end disaster. Soon after the mouse dream, she dreamt of a cracked freezer (Chapter Three, pp. 94–97) which the repairman did not acknowledge. The cracked freezer was an image of truncated disaster. Apparently, Lynn did not feel that I dealt with a streak of madness.

Her thoughts turned to her father. His quiet warmth had a frozen aspect. He was too quiet and still, like a corpse. Lynn did not like his touch. At times he unpredictably yelled and screamed. He was a kind of cracked freezer, just as her mother was a kind of fire. Lynn froze or became overheated or flooded—ice, fire, water. She felt hysterical. She would clam up or yell like her father or be bossy, manipulative and emotionally demanding like her mother. No wonder it was a relief to go blank!

Only after her cracked father became important in therapy did Lynn's urge to become pregnant blossom. A madness and deficiency in the father aspect of her psyche prevented her from becoming a mother. Her repulsion for her father froze her and made her mad. His inadequacy in regulating feelings left her with a similar deficiency. Her repulsion tried to protect her. It toned down unmanageable stimulation by keeping things distant. Instinctive repulsion was commandeered psychically to regulate reactions against parental deficiencies. Unfortunately, defensive overuse of repulsion become frozen madness, too. It slows down or stops psychic hemorrhage but, like a tourniquet gone mad, ties psyche into knots.

To get pregnant was part of Lynn's life drive. It is what she wanted but had been unable to achieve until she worked with the cracked freezer, her crazy father, a broken psychic function. She brought psychic disasters into therapy so that she could reshape herself in terms of her main lifeline.

Reshaping the Self

Love lit Lynn's life and gave her strength and faith to come through. The problem was not love; rather it was the personalities of her parents and husband, as well as her own personality. The love that lit her heart was coated by reactive shell within shell. Love did its work through personality tendencies that worked against it.

The people around Lynn were strangers to themselves, not up to the processes that constituted them. The psyche was not adequate to itself. Lynn made her way as a stranger in her own psyche and linked herself with symbols of the best she could muster. Therapy ended when she connected herself with a living embodiment of heart, the essence of what made life worthwhile. With her baby, she had a chance to unknot herself more radically. Having a baby was a victory of faith.

The shock of therapy was the truth that it was no easier to reshape herself than reshape the things she hated outside herself. She was constrained by twists in her own personality. Inner-outer realities reinforced one another.

A gift of therapy was Lynn's discovery of the ability to become shapeless. Lynn could drop between lines of self and system to a realm of stunning shapelessness until there was nothing left but an opening-closing heart. At the place of opening-closing one feels fresh. Motherhood accelerated the process of opening. With a child, Lynn would know permeability-oppositionalism in new ways. Therapy and life worked together so that Lynn's personality, vocation, marriage, motherhood became part of the larger shapeless reshaping process, part of heart's labor from trauma to trauma, joy to joy.

Chapter Seven

Primary Process and the Wound That Never Heals

Different schools of depth psychology develop different languages for the wound that never heals. We are wounded beings and much depends not only on the severity of our wounds but on how we process or fail to process them.

There are many ways of relating to wounds. One may turn them into blessings. One may wrestle with them. One may go into wounds, explore them, try to go through them, heal them, learn about them. One may get lost in wounds or drown in wounds. Wounds can be traps or springboards, challenges or simply tragedies. One may fly above them. I have a patient currently who has spent his life flying, looking for a bit of unwounded territory to land on. He does not remember the last time he touched earth.

All wounds are part of one great wound. I think we have a sense of being wounded on which all wounds feed. We grow around our wounds. What we call character may be ways of organizing our selves around and beyond wounds in characteristic ways. A sense of bitterness, loss, or self-pity signals a background wound we take for granted, live with, and transcend in ordinary daily living.

Several generations of psychoanalysts have put together a growing picture of the wounded self: birth trauma, annihilation anxiety, separation-intrusion anxieties, castration anxiety. Development is riddled with terrors, barriers, mortifications. Winnicott (1974) depicted a host of "primitive agonies" clustering around loss of self and orientation and the sense of realness.

Freud's dream book (1900) brimmed with descriptions of wounded ambition, slights, blows to self-esteem, wounded wishes. His work grew into a catalogue of wounded desires. Development moved not only from desire to desire and pleasure to pleasure, but also from wound to wound. Freud gave validity to the hysteric's expressive language. Phrases like "a blow to the face" or "stab in the heart" were more than vain exaggerations; they portrayed affective truth, moments of painful sensitivity (Freud, 1900, 1905, 1915, 1920).

One of Freud's (1900, 1911; Breuer & Freud, 1895) great contributions was connecting the language of dreams with wounded wishes. This moved beyond simply honoring the power of wishing in motivation and thinking. Freud delineated a different style of thinking in dream work than the mixture of logic and common sense that, supposedly, dominated waking thought.

Dream work makes freer use of objects, parts of objects, and elements of space and time than does waking consciousness. Multiple objects can be melded, single objects broken apart and redistributed. Freud's dream book traces ways in which daily injuries find expression in dreams. At night, the dreamer avenges slights that paralyzed or flew by him during the day. A dream may try to right the balance, repair or undo injury, get the dreamer back on top again. That so many dreams are frightening suggests that our power to process injury successfully is weak. We are not very good at processing wounds.

Freud associates injury with self-deception. We deal with wounds by lying to ourselves. When we get angry enough at ourselves for lying, when our lies become too suffocating, the truth explodes, often destructively.

We hunger for emotional truth, but we are also lying beings. Even when speaking truth we may be dimly aware of unconsciously lying. Others all too easily spot the lie we try to hide from ourselves. There are also truths in lies. Our attempts to polarize lies and truth have not yielded overwhelmingly happy results. Yet to give up on truth courts psychosocial collapse.

What we need are new and better ways of processing the mixture of truth and lies we feel we are. Truth can kill. Lies can poison. Lies can be fun, even creative. Truth can free. We can be wounded by truth and wounded by lies. A workable mixture of both can be healing. We are still in infancy in our ability to deal with the endless permutation and condensation-displacement of truth-lies that are part of existence.

Freud's distinction between primary process (dream language) and secondary process (waking logic, common sense) draws on the romantic distinction between analytic consciousness and intuition/imagination. The modern poet and artist vacillate between mythopoetic and analytic states of mind (e.g., Barfield, 1964; Ehrenzweig, 1971). All materials, states of mind, and capacities are grist for creative work.

It is no accident that so many myths and poems are concerned with catastrophe, whether disaster and violence associated with beginnings and endings or love wounds. Primary process takes seriously successes and failures that pack the workplace. Freud's analyses of his own dreams were obsessed with wounded ambition.

Freud suggested that wounds separated in time feed one another. Current wounds united with wounds going back through the years to earliest childhood. There is a connection, a flow back and forth between present and past. Through condensation-displacement, apparently disconnected wounds come together, and wounds that seem to have little to do with one another resonate in common. This is so not only with time but with diverse areas of experience. Freud envisioned professional wounds and love wounds as branches of a single great river, its source in infancy and its end in death.

We are beings prone to affect explosions and are wounded by our emotional violence. The screams of infancy never die out. They echo in the background of our beings. What might have been a scream in infancy bursts through a gun aimed at a current symbol or agent of wounds. One wounds an imaginary or real wound-maker. One makes a killing in a business deal. One wounds, or heals, society through political machinations. One hears the scream running through the social fabric. The comedian turns scream to laughter, and when he or she does it well, we say, "What a scream!"

An element of lasting value in Freud's work is that he depicted, or tried to depict, ways in which we process affective intensity. Primary process begins the processing of affect, especially bits of catastrophic impacts that threaten to overwhelm equipment and break down functioning. Processes of condensation, displacement, symbolization, et al., funnel affect into dream work. Affect-charged images and primitive narrative give rise to further psychic elaboration. Bits of catastrophic moments become parts of unending cultural associations and are given new meaning in art, literature, mystical experience, science, and everyday life.

Dreams are reservoirs of wounds. Very often they do not succeed in processing wounds in growth-producing ways. They keep flashing images of where and how personality is stuck. They signal points of breakdown. It is important to note that it is not merely secondary process logic, common sense, and cognition that fail to process the wound that does not heal and the point of breakdown. Primary process also breaks down or becomes defective. Metabolizing affect goes on from the bottom up, as well as from the top down. No amount of secondary process compensation makes up for primary process not working well.

The therapist becomes a kind of auxiliary primary processor (Eigen, 1986, 1992, 1995b). He or she tries to metabolize the patient's stuck points, especially breakdowns in ability to process catastrophic impacts. Therapy is akin to a primary process gymnasium. The therapist's processing ability is inadequate, too, but therapy helps make room for processing ability to grow. In this regard, therapist and patient grow together.

There are catastrophes about which nothing can be said except that they are irreducible, final, horrific. Nevertheless, the ability to process catastrophic elements of experience develops. There is no way of knowing ahead of time what must be left outside the range of processing ability, which pockets of despair are metabolizable and which will last to the end of our days. Perhaps a great deal of what happens in a lifetime is beyond processing.

For thousands of years, humanity has been trying to develop effective ways to process wounds, terrors, joys, points of breakdown, points of maximum intensity. Art, music, literature, religion, philosophy, science, political and social institutions all attempt to express, investigate, reshape, and process consequences of our sensitivity in workable and meaningful ways. They strive to stimulate growth of processing ability and, at the same time, function as partial indices of the success or failure of growth processes. Psychotherapy is a relative newcomer to the experience-processing scene. It contributes an element not quite addressed by other agents of processing—a new, deep, idiosyncratic, person-to-person interaction aimed at catalyzing, nurturing, and channeling growth processes.

We are trying to learn something about living with ourselves. Processing attempts are limited, in a sense failures. We never fully process the wounds we are or become all that we can be. Yet even limited success in fragmentary bits of processing ability make big differences in the quality and direction of lives.[1]

Trauma, Snakes, and Devils

In a sense, Les's entire therapy involved a kind of sparring between us that stimulated growth in his primary processing ability. He needed a sparring partner, but not at the superficial ego levels he was used to. To an extent, he thrived on a semi-oppositional relationship. However, he was not used to talking about his dreams, dreads, longings, and hopes with an oppositional other that was basically on his side. Moreover, he could not conceive of an oppositional other that supported processes that functioned in his dreams.

Les got close to people by fighting, and he needed to do that with me. However, most of his fighting went around the same old circles. Sometimes fighting cleared the air or succeeded in making contact. At other times, it enabled him to create distance between himself and his wounds and get away from feeling entrapped. Sometimes the fighting was just plain fun; at other times it was unbearably horrible. Les's wife, mother, children,

---

[1]Among colleagues whose views are related to my own are Nelson, 1967; Rycroft, 1968; Noy, 1968; Ehrenzweig, 1971; Matte-Blanco, 1975; Robbins, 1980; Grotstein, 1981; McDougall, 1985; Green, 1986; Milner, 1987; Benjamin, 1988; Ulman & Brothers, 1988; Kurtz, 1989; Schwartz-Salant, 1989; Fromm & Smith, 1989; Ghent, 1990; Seinfeld, 1991; Bollas, 1992; Boris, 1993; Ehrenfeld, 1993; Phillips, 1994; Ogden, 1994; Epstein, 1995; Lifschitz, 1995.

and Les himself caused one another much pain by battling, often opening old wounds and inflicting new ones.
Fighting with me, by contrast, enabled Les to get closer
to the wounds his fighting grew out of and kept reopen-
ing. With me he could voice more fully his sense of
injury without fearing retaliation.

Our relationship, more than others he was used to,
was better able to tolerate his expressions of frustration,
rage, injury, and self-pity without my needing anything
from him. In Les's life, anger usually triggered hurt or
anger in return. Indeed, Les was long made uncomfortable by my not reacting in trigger-crazy fashion to his
angry, hurt, demanding, or needy self. His moods and
feelings impacted on me, and I stayed with their impact
as best I could.

Frequently during sessions I would sit with his
impact and let my feelings, together with imaginings and
thoughts based on these feelings, grow and mature. This
often maddened Les because he thought I was doing
nothing. He seemed to want me to boss him as his
mother did, but, at the same time, was terrified that I
might actually do so. The idea that I was merely "feeling" him or thinking about him drove him mad. Yet it
also intrigued him and made him feel important in a new
way, and he kept coming back for more. In her own way,
Les's wife played a similar role since she had him inside
her, too, and loved him. She simply lacked the expertise
and distance to enable his ability to tolerate his own states
grow past a certain point. She had too much invested in
their relationship not to jump in the ring and start swing-
ing wildly.

In addition, I was the only one in Les's life who enjoyed listening to his dreams on a fairly consistent basis and who had ideas about them that stimulated feelings about himself he had not been able to get to or stay with for long. I suspect having contact with someone who valued and supported dream processes enabled Les to produce his first extended, nearly coherent dream of himself on a journey, sailing the seas of life and the unconscious and coming through a variety of dangers one encounters in oneself and others.

For most of his life, Les feared dreaming because his dreams tended to be nightmarish. They often ended with threatened disasters. They did not contain much complexity or buildup of tensions, but seemed to rush towards some horrible end. His dream of a semi-heroic journey lasted longer than most he recalled and contained more diverse elements: an unpredictable sea that could be violent or smooth as glass, a guide, boats, friends, relatives, poisonous snakes, a mixture of danger and affection. The longer duration and the elevated diversity of this dream offered me some indication that his psyche could contain a bit more tension before collapsing.

In addition to bad-good, mother-father, wife-therapist, children-self and all the ambivalent (love-hate) relationships in his life, the dream reflected the simple fact that psychic life is turbulent (Bion, 1976). Many people seem to feel that if they were "better" their lives would be less turbulent. Les blamed his tumultuous ups and downs on his pathology, his "sick self." He felt that if he had not been so victimized by parental injury he would now be calmer, more secure, more imperturbable. To some extent, he might have been right. Yet fluctuations in emotions may be as natural as fluctuations in weather.

The result of Les blaming his emotional swings on his pathology and parents was that he ended up also blaming himself. If he were a better or different person, then the sea would be calm. Throughout his life, Les tried to control his emotional storminess, only to feel all the worse when a temper storm broke out. Neither blaming self or others nor trying to control emotional pressures provided real relief. The new element in the journey dream was that storminess and poison were parts of a larger journey. Les was developing a bigger picture of life, but he did not let himself know it yet. His dream life, the index of psychic foundations, lived it before he did.

The larger journey included strivings to control both unpredictable and uncontrollable elements, attachments, separations, overall movement, direction, challenges, and a mixture of failure and success. Aspects of nature, culture, and human relationships intermixed. My view is that Les's unconscious had grown to the extent that it could contain broader combinations of dangers and possibilities. Of course, this meant that *he* had grown to the point where he could produce and live through such a dream experience. One would think his relationships with people in waking life were growing also, that he could absorb a wider range of feeling states with others and himself.

Until this point, Les did not have an unconscious that could cushion or protect itself from its own productions. All his life he terrified himself with his nightmares, which spilled over into daytime anxieties. I believe that through experiencing me absorb and work on his emotional states (partially process them through my imagining, reveries, etc.), Les felt what it was like to have an unconscious that could work on states it needed to produce.

He needed to produce representations of wounds and wounding processes and the horror he felt. He needed to catalogue life's traumas. His psyche was alive and truthful enough to come up with images of its wounds and dreads, but through therapy he received support deep enough to enable more psychic processing to evolve. His dreams could begin to connect and amplify a variety of experiences through more complex narratives and begin to encompass some of the sense of injury that had previously tyrannized and flooded them.

If water represents the unconscious or birth or emotional life, what are poisonous snakes? Snakes can symbolize unconscious wisdom (Eigen, 1986), but there are Biblical associations of the snake with the devil, with poisonous lies. Did the snake in the garden speak the truth or did it lie? Or both? Does its truth-lie function depend on context and viewpoint? References to poison must be taken seriously.

When I was with Les, I could feel ways in which he felt poisoned and poisoned himself. If poison came from a parent, Les was a carrier of it now, like vampire creates vampire. We are inserted in structures that have poisonous aspects, just as we find ourselves part of a universe that has radioactive processes. The challenge is not to pin the tail on the poisoner but to discover ways of working with the poisons we find.

The fact that Les's waking life gradually improved and his dreaming life became more complex and able to sustain tensions, suggested that real growth was occurring. A connection was growing between the dreaming and waking self so that each did not have to guard against and undermine the other (Scott, 1975). Unconscious and conscious life were working together. The change in Les's dream life suggested that he was growing in primary process ability, facilitating meaningful work with the wounds and dreads that immobilized him.

A paradoxical result of this work is that the distinction between conscious and unconscious processes begins to blur. Poisons spread throughout the whole psyche, both the conscious and the unconscious. A poisoned-poisonous psyche is not confined to one or another function or set of processes. For example, there is conscious and unconscious lying and conscious-unconscious use and misuse of truth. I believe Les's dream began to absorb and encompass this complexity. His dream depicted a larger situation with more diverse elements than Les was used to holding together in a single view. Les's dreaming experience was stimulating growth of waking consciousness, as well as vice versa.

We can see this growth carried forward much later in Les's therapy. The Neville the Devil dream holds even more intense threats of disaster in a broader, more complex framework than Les's earlier boat dream, although the simple hero structure is maintained. Here we have a devil that drugs people, does harm to them, threatens abandonment and annihilation anxieties, has a piercing mental ego (eyes) and powerful body ego (the great fight). In addition to the dream's overall complexity, many of its parts had inner complexities (the intricate room, multi-functional devil, reference to orality and breathing). If the overall structure was a simple story of threat and triumph, the increment of emotional intensity that the dream sustained was palpable.

To be sure, there are advantages to snakes over a more formal devil. The former are less ritualized, closer to nature. But the fusion of the many (snakes) into one (Neville the Devil) enabled the psyche to pack more tension into less space and concentrate energy in a tighter drama (Kluger & Kluger, 1984). This economy of form and energy enabled Les to begin moving through stuck points into the wider stream of life. He could rely more on unconscious processing rather than be paralyzed in a state of fearful vigilance.

Fire, Ice, Babies

In previous chapters, we discussed the movement in Lynn's dream images from a fire in the basement to a broken freezer in a refrigerator, suggesting difficulties both below and above (body-self/mental-self). These changing images reflected and emphasized shifts of concern in unconscious processing.

The fire in the basement suggested something was wrong from the ground up. The unconscious could not contain itself. The fire spread from bottom to above, affecting higher mental functions. Lynn could not trust her unconscious to do the work it was required to do. Whatever was wrong in the foundation spread throughout the building. Her entire psyche was affected by pressing difficulties.

At the same time, her unconscious *was* doing the work it needed to do. It was signaling that something was "off," that there were disturbances too hot for her to handle, that professional help (firemen, therapist) needed to be called in. Her dream work signaled that her psyche was burning and that she lacked ability to process her disturbances effectively.

Dreams often portray difficulties that the psyche has with unconscious processing. Damaged or undeveloped primary processing capacity is frequently reflected in dreams. While a dream portrays problems with self and others (in Lynn's case anger at husband, boss, parents, sibling, therapist, self), it also mirrors holes, deficits, damage in psychic processing.

As was the case with Les, Lynn never was in a situation where her psyche received the support and atmosphere her primary processing capacity needed for fuller evolution. It necessarily tripped over its own work because it was as concerned with portraying its own incapacity and damage as it was in fingering difficulties with internal and external objects. And, like Les, Lynn needed to form a partly combative relationship with me, since she was used to fighting with people. Although this tendency toward combativeness never left her, Lynn also felt a need to get beyond it. She felt her combativeness saved her in daily life but kept her away from herself. In therapy she could feel me feeling her, or wanting to feel her, and this added fuel to her wish to see what life might be like if she became less defensive.

In fact, Lynn's daily life required combativeness if she were to survive at work or with her family and husband. She developed the trait her practical life needed—the life her combativeness needed. In either case, she and her current life fit each other fairly well. However, the result was that she did not fit her self. She felt there was more to both life and her self. Therapy was her attempt to grope for this *more*.

That Lynn could dream of a fire in the basement meant to me that therapy was very real to her and that she would make very real use of it. She was able to show me that something was wrong at bottom and that it affected her entire life. Yet her building and life and marriage survived the danger. She brought the dream to show the depths of her feeling that something was wrong, but by the act of doing so implicitly suggested enough faith that we could work with her problems.

As time went on, Lynn revealed to me that something was wrong with the top, as well as the bottom. Neither top nor bottom were working well enough for her to trust her own capacities. The freezer compartment was broken and threatened to flood. The cold flood moved from top down, as the fire spread from bottom up. Lynn was deeply afraid of her thoughts and feelings. She feared her capacity to use her head, heart, and genitals was deeply damaged and that her thoughts, emotions, and passions would further damage her.

She was experiencing a sense of damage that ran through her psyche and that went together with feeling damaging. Yet she felt compelled to seek an experience that went deeper than any sense of damage she conceived.

While therapy provided Lynn with the supportive atmosphere that allowed her to delve deeper, it must be pointed out that Lynn sought therapy for that very purpose. Something inside her was propelling her past herself, into therapy, to reach pay dirt. Thus, it is not enough to say that therapy/therapist enabled Lynn to tap new regions of experiencing when that is precisely what Lynn unconsciously came for. Lynn called therapy into being; it was not simply the other way around.

It would seem then that there was something at work in Lynn that unconsciously knew what she needed for growth and self-repair while preserving the life she valued (Eigen, 1993; Jung, 1958). In the face of damaged processing ability, a tacit urge to subtend the damage in some measure won out.

Lynn's therapy culminated in dreams of giving birth, displaced onto others (Chapter Three, pp. 101–105). This seemed to represent more than Lynn subtending or transcending her damaged self. I believe that it symbolized actual growth in primary processing ability and a distinct evolution of dream work. This did not mean all damage was repaired or that disaster anxiety was not omnipresent (Eigen, 1995a). The birth dream contained many tensions and anxieties. But life processes move on with and through disaster anxieties.

Neither fire nor ice stopped Lynn's generativity; indeed, they added to it. They are part of the full range of human emotionality and use of self. There is no question that Lynn could not have "righted" herself without therapy. Her life would have eaten her up. She was on the brink of a downward spiral that would have been destructive. The fire would have become too much for her as its devastating fury mounted. Similarly, reactive coldness would have become intolerable; the hotter Lynn became, the colder she would have to get. Yet, with help, Lynn became more secure in her generativity in all aspects of her life.

One must credit therapy for providing a place where reshaping processes bear fruit for many individuals. The therapist may be a new other, an ally who sides with inner growth in ways that others in one's life cannot. The therapist provides a nurturing atmosphere, an attitudinal framework, and significant emotional transmissions that enable and encourage a person to evolve. The therapist also brings poisons into the equation, since no one is free of toxins. Yet as the therapist works on processing the patient's impact, takes the patient into his mental world, and lives with the patient as a real and inner object (with whatever mixtures of poisons/damage/health), the individual may be stimulated to do the same with him or herself, thereby linking up with his or her evolution.

Both Lynn and Les tapped a generative dimension in their beings that had been endangered. While for them therapy was a necessary condition for this to happen, it was not sufficient. One must also credit whatever prompted them to seek therapy and to keep at it until a reshaping process that felt right enough to embrace took hold. I think there is in us a mute sense and faith in reshaping processes that go very deep, and, if we are lucky, we mate with conditions that mediate these processes. We are capable of struggling through eons of unrecognizability in our quest, and may even become capable of creating by ourselves the conditions we need.

Wells on Fire: Wounds and Therapy

Wounds of childhood are wells on fire. We cap them as we can and harden around them. Sometimes we develop colorful exoskeletons. We may try to suffocate the fire and sometimes nearly succeed. The fire may become a shriek. Hitler's life was an extended shriek. His concentration camps were images of his own shriek, for which he substituted the shrieks of others. They join the shriek that runs through history.

The scream of life is a scream of pain. A baby's scream can signal relief because it tells us the baby is alive. The link between suffering and aliveness is inextricable. It is an all too small step to slide into the need to provoke that scream to feel aliveness.

The link between suffering and aliveness is an intrinsic part of growth processes. If one speaks of birth trauma, one might also speak of fertilization trauma or embryonic growth trauma. Sperm bombardment, implosive-explosive entry into egg, wave after wave of sequential development, moments of fetal distress—the womb is perfect only in fantasy. Perhaps thumb sucking in the womb is a reflex to regulate stress, an active attempt at self-soothing, a spontaneous discovery of how to produce pleasure, an attempt to close the circuit and feel whole.

What sorts of being are outcomes of radioactive processes, electromagnetic fields, and explosive-cooling processes that splatter and order systems of solar bodies? Unseen universes make up our bodies. The material universe is malleable beyond expectation. Psychic rigidities baffle us.

It is difficult to imagine a universe without pain or what we would be like without the capacity for pain. Some individuals grow so numb with pain that they try to recapture the capacity for pain through the suffering they cause others. There are murderers who need to see, or at least imagine, the pain in their victim's face. The wounded look of the victim keeps the murderer's sense of fragility alive. Pain is a constant—the pain of the infant, the pain of the child, the pain of the teenager, the pain of passage into adulthood, the pain of the adult.

The story of Job has significance today because it mirrors the contraction-expansion of personality that goes on throughout a lifetime. Job contracts to the *pain point*, the place where there is nothing but pain. The pleasure he has in his body, his family, his flocks is taken away. The story dramatizes this movement in external, common-sense terms. The losses are real: real people, real animals, real body.

One may also read the story of Job in psychological terms. The animals, family, and body are expressions of an alive-and-well self, the self in plenitude. When trauma is severe enough and the wounding great enough, the alive-and-well self moves through pain and torment towards death. Job becomes pure pain, torment, living hell. One wonders how much he can bear.

Job's paradox is that at the point of maximum intensity, a breakthrough occurs: he sees God. Pain is transformed to joy. A moment of expansion begins. All is lost, then heaven opens. New flocks, new family, and healed body express the expansive moment. Life is renewed. Expansion-contraction, pain-joy, the opening-closing heart—it is a never-ending story.

In therapy, Les and Lynn contracted to pain points. They did this repeatedly over extended periods of time. They did not do this in an absolute, total way, as Job did. Their daily lives went on as usual. But in therapy their wounds could speak in a more concentrated way than in daily life. The wells on fire could burn brightly during the therapy hour without consuming their entire lives.

Therapy encourages one to gravitate to the thing that is "off" in order to refashion it. Something in the self feels wrong. The self incessantly struggles to reshape itself. Therapy helps the personality reshape itself in more expedient ways. Les and Lynn had the sagacity to seek help when they felt themselves closing around their wounds to the point that their sense of inner constriction became intolerable. They sought help before it became impossible to reshape the self in a way that would be gratifying and fulfilling.

Wounds harden people. Wounds can turn individuals into killers of themselves and others. Some of the wounded become unable to change. In many individuals, there may be areas of hardened wounds that are beyond reach. Luckily, Les and Lynn never lost contact with areas of fragility. They were able to use therapy to rework themselves in ways that included fresh patternings of hardening-fragility.

Les and Lynn became better versions of themselves, in part, because wounds they despaired of reaching entered communication processes. Simply speaking about wounds is not enough to heal them; such expectation is unrealistic, too much to ask. But speaking about what one despaired of reaching brings its own joy. One resonates with joyous appreciation when therapy helps uncover wounds that one secretly believed to be outside the realm of human communication.

Therapy provides a place where energy and meaning in the personality can begin to flow more freely. In time, individuals discover unexpected pleasures in getting to what feels wrong and becoming partners in the reshaping processes. Joy seeks core wounds with a healing passion; there is real satisfaction in going through experiences that one could not previously acknowledge or stay with. Therapy supports therapist and patient alike in melding areas of wounded hardening with moments of opening. People like Lynn and Les demonstrate that not everything can or needs to change in order for miracles of transformation to be achieved. One develops a taste and feel for reworking self, a need for personality realignment, so that the capacity to reshape the self becomes part of everyday living.

Bibliography

Balint, M. (1968). *The Basic Fault*. London: Tavistock.

Barfield, O. (1964). *Poetic Diction: A Study of Meaning*. New York: McGraw-Hill.

Benjamin, J. (1988). *The Bonds of Love*. New York: Pantheon Books.

Bion, W. R. (1970). *Attention and Interpretation*. London: Karnac, 1984.

—— (1976). Emotional turbulence. In F. Bion (Ed.), *Clinical Seminars and Other Works*, pp. 295–305. London: Karnac Books.

Bollas, C. (1992). *Being a Character*. New York: Hill and Wang.

Boris, H. (1993). *Passions of the Mind*. New York: New York University Press.

Breuer, J., & Freud, S. (1895). Studies on hysteria. *Standard Edition*, 2:3–309. London: Hogarth Press, 1955.

Buber, M. (1958). *I and Thou*. New York: Charles Scribner's Sons.

Corrigan, E. G., & Gordon, P-E. (1995). *The Mind Object*. Northvale, NJ: Jason Aronson.

Ehrenfeld, D. (1993). *The Intimate Edge*. Northvale, NJ: Jason Aronson.

Ehrenzweig, A. (1971). *The Hidden Order of Art*. Berkeley: University of California Press.

Eigen, M. (1974). On pre-oedipal castration anxiety. *International Review of Psychoanalysis*, 1:489–498.

—— (1981). Maternal abandonment threats, mind-body relations and suicidal wishes. *Journal of the American Academy of Psychoanalysis*, 9:561–582.

—— (1986). *The Psychotic Core*. Northvale, NJ: Jason Aronson.
—— (1991). A flying phobia: Mind-body splits and individuation. In E. Thorne & S. H. Schaye (Eds.), *Psychoanalysis Today: A Case Book*, pp. 133–154. Springfield, IL: Charles C Thomas.
—— (1992). *Coming Through the Whirlwind*. Wilmette, IL: Chiron Publications.
—— (1993). *The Electrified Tightrope*. Northvale, NJ: Jason Aronson.
—— (1995a). Disaster anxiety. In J. A. Travers & E. M. Stern (Eds.), *Psychotherapy and the Dangerous Patient*, pp. 59–76. Binghamton, NY: The Haworth Press.
—— (1995b). Primary process and shock. *Create*, Vol. 5, in press.
Elkin, H. (1972). On selfhood and the development of ego structures in infancy. *Psychoanalytic Review*, 59:389–416.
Epstein, M. (1995). *Thoughts without a Thinker: Psychotherapy from a Buddhist Perspective*. New York: Basic Books.
Federn, P. (1957). *Ego Psychology and the Psychoses*. London: Maresfield Reprints.
Freud, S. (1895). Project for a scientific psychology. In M. Bonaparte, A. Freud, & E. Kris (Eds.), *The Origins of Psychoanalysis: Letters to Wilhelm Fliess, Drafts and Notes*, 1887–1902, pp. 356–445. New York: Basic Books, 1954.
—— (1900). The interpretation of dreams. *Standard Edition*, 4/5: 1–361. London: Hogarth Press, 1953.
—— (1905). Three essays on the theory of sexuality. *Standard Edition*, 7:125–245. London: Hogarth Press, 1953.
—— (1911). Formulations on the two principles of mental functioning. *Standard Edition*, 12:218–226. London: Hogarth Press, 1958.
—— (1915). Instincts and their vicissitudes. *Standard Edition*, 14: 117–140. London: Hogarth Press, 1957.
—— (1920). Beyond the pleasure principle. *Standard Edition*, 18: 1–64. London: Hogarth Press, 1955.
Fromm, M. G., & Smith, B. L. (Eds.) (1989). *The Facilitating Environment: Clinical Applications of Winnicott's Theory*. Madison, CT: International Universities Press.
Ghent, E. (1990). Masochism, submission, surrender. *Contemporary Psychoanalysis*, 26:108–136.
Green, A. (1986). *On Private Madness*. London: Hogarth Press and the Institute of Psycho-Analysis.

Bibliography

Grotstein, J. (1981). *Splitting and Projective Identification*. Northvale, NJ: Jason Aronson.

Jung, C. G. (1958). The transcendent function. *Collected Works*, 8:67–91. Princeton, NJ: Princeton University Press, 1969.

Kluger, R. S., & Kluger, H. Y. (1984). Evil in dreams: A Jungian view. In M. C. Nelson & M. Eigen (Eds.), *Evil: Self and Culture*, pp. 162–169. New York: Human Sciences Press.

Kohut, H. (1971). *The Analysis of Self*. New York: International Universities Press.

Kurtz, S. (1989). *The Art of Unknowing*. Northvale, NJ: Jason Aronson.

Lacan, J. (1977). *Ecrits* (A. Sheridan, Trans.). New York: Norton.

Levinas, E. (1969). *Totality and Infinity* (A. Lingis, Trans.). Pittsburgh: Duquesne University.

Lifschitz, M. (1995). *Freedom from Memory, Desire, and Understanding*. New York: Irvington Publishers.

Luijpen, W. A. (1960). *Existential Phenomenology*. Pittsburgh: Duquesne University.

Masson, J. (Ed.) (1985). *The Complete Letters of Sigmund Freud to Wilhelm Fliess: 1887–1904*. Cambridge, MA: Harvard University Press.

Matte-Blanco, I. (1975). *The Unconscious as Infinite Sets*. London: Duckworth Press.

McDougall, J. (1985). *Theaters of the Mind*. New York: Basic Books.

Meltzer, D. (1973). *Sexual States of Mind*. Perthshire, Scotland: Clunie Press.

—— (1977). *The Kleinian Development*. Perthshire, Scotland: Clunie Press.

Milner, M. (1987). *The Suppressed Madness of Sane Men*. London: Tavistock.

Nelson, M. C. (1967). On the therapeutic redirection of energy and affects. *International Journal of Psycho-Analysis*, 48.

Noy, P. (1968). The development of musical ability. *The Psychoanalytic Study of the Child*. New York: International Universities Press.

Ogden, T. (1994). *Subjects of Analysis*. Northvale, NJ: Jason Aronson.

Phillips, A. (1994). *On Flirtation*. London: Faber and Faber.

Reich, W. (1949). *Character Analysis*. New York: Farrar, Strauss & Cudahy.

Robbins, A. (Ed.) (1980). *Expressive Therapy*. New York: Human Sciences Press.

Rycroft, C. (1968). *Imagination and Reality*. New York: International Universities Press.

Schwartz-Salant, N. (1989). *The Borderline Personality: Vision and Healing*. Wilmette, IL: Chiron Publications.

Scott, W. C. M. (1975). Remembering sleep and dreams. *International Review of Psycho-Analysis*, 2:253–354.

Seinfeld, J. (1991). *The Empty Core*. Northvale, NJ: Jason Aronson.

Stern, D. (1977). *The First Relationship*. Boston: Harvard University Press.

Ulman, R. B., & Brothers, D. (1988). *The Shattered Self*. Hillsdale, NJ: Analytic Press.

Winnicott, D. W. (1974). Fear of breakdown. *International Review of Psycho-Analysis*, 1:103–107.